BUSES
YEARBOOK 2001

Edited by STEWART J. BROWN

Ian Allan PUBLISHING

First published 2000

ISBN 0 7110 2724 2

Published by Ian Allan Publishing

an imprint of Ian Allan Publishing Ltd, Terminal House, Shepperton, Surrey TW17 8AS.
Printed by Ian Allan Printing Ltd, Riverdene Business Park, Hersham, Surrey KT12 4RG.

Code: 0008/F2

Front cover:
West Midlands supported local bus maker MCW when it launched its integral Metrobus, becoming the biggest user of the type outside London – The last years of the MCW, page 51. *Stewart J. Brown*

Back cover, top:
Chance encounter: an early Dennis Dart with Duple Dartline body in the fleet of Norfolk Green – Luck breaks, page 3. *Peter Rowlands*

Back cover, bottom:
Stagecoach has been cascading buses from its London fleets to less taxing provincial operations. A former East London Wright-bodied Dart is seen with Stagecoach South – Capital cascade, page 41.

Title page:
Repatriated to Britain in the 1980s, a former Lisbon AEC seen at Sandtoft – Turning the clock back, page 107. *Michael Fowler*

Below right:
Leyland Atlanteans are fast disappearing from British bus fleets – Late developer, page 31. *Gavin Booth*

Contents

LUCKY BREAKS
Peter Rowlands   3

GORGEOUS GAS OR JUST HOT AIR?
Alan Millar   11

A CENTURY OF MANCHESTER'S BUSES
Reg Wilson   19

THE END OF SMT
Billy Nicol   27

LATE DEVELOPER
Gavin Booth   31

CAPITAL CASCADE
Stephen Morris   41

THE LAST YEARS OF MCW
Stewart J. Brown   51

PACKING 'EM IN!
David Wayman   65

TRAVELS THROUGH ASIA
Michael H. C. Baker   73

ORKNEY OVERTURE
Roy Marshall   83

FORTY YEARS OF TOURING
Geoff Mills   89

THE YELLOW DOG AND THE FLOATING BRIDGE
Robert E. Jowitt   97

TURNING THE CLOCK BACK
Michael Fowler   107

SAVER SEVENTY-SEVEN
Oliver Howarth   113

THE TWIN-STEER BEDFORD
Kevin Lane   123

LUCKY

BREAKS

Prologue

Picture a drab weekday morning in the early 1980s (you'll have to, because I no longer have the evidence). I'm driving eastwards out of Bristol on a roundabout return journey to London. My route takes me past the old Bristol Commercial Vehicles factory at Brislington, where Bristol bus chassis were made for so many years. Bus production has already stopped here for ever, but the site has not yet been turned over to some new use.

I can see some workmen gathered by the gateway on the left and as I approach, it becomes evident that they're carefully removing the large metal 'Bristol' nameplate from the wall – one that picks out the familiar Bristol scroll logo in three dimensions. Marvelling at the coincidence of having arrived here at this precise moment, I pull over, grab my camera and photograph them at their sorry task. Satisfied that they're taking care of the nameplate, not simply scrapping it, I return to my car and drive on.

Taking bus photographs requires knowledge and patience, but it can also involve a modicum of luck. Peter Rowlands owns up to some of his more fortunate catches.

Back at home, I submit one of the pictures to a weekly transport magazine, whose deputy editor declares himself happy to print it. 'It makes us look as if we've got people everywhere,' he says.

Those words have resounded in my memory over the years. They seem to articulate one of the most familiar experiences of many bus photographers. It is to exploit the happy coincidences of life; to make it appear that some piece of good fortune was intended; to be able to

1991: The first London Metrobus

Top:
1988: The last Routemaster

Above:
1980: FRM1

present a chance photograph as though it were carefully planned and inevitable.

To those more conscientious photographers who spend whole days planning and setting up one picture, I apologise now. You have my respect. I speak for the rest of us – grateful for the less predictable prizes life offers.

I'm sorry to say I no longer have those valedictory Bristol pictures; they passed to my employer at the time. I do however have many others that might seem to have been carefully contrived, but actually owe more to luck than judgement. Time to confess.

First ...

Something I could never understand about London Metrobuses was why London Transport specified a very wide front destination panel for them, when in practice it never used the full width of the display. This was doubly puzzling, since the five prototypes had the narrower display panel used on the DMS-class Fleetlines that they superseded. What was wrong with that?

At any rate, the five kept their distinctive look right through their lives, standing out from all their later counterparts. Even less reason to feel any great achievement in photographing them, perhaps; especially as they could often be found waiting at the bus stand at Marble Arch, easy prey to even the least conscientious photographer. I've photographed them in various guises at various times, there and elsewhere; even become insouciant enough to let them pass unheeded.

Yet there's always a sense of achievement in getting a good shot of the first of the batch. I know my collection would be incomplete without them. So what if I've never once gone looking for them in my life? I'm not telling anyone, are you?

Last ...

Yes, yes; everyone has a picture of RML2760, numerically the last London Routemaster. I know I've got mine. It's not as if it's all that difficult to track down. As I write, it's still in daily service, nowadays with Stagecoach East London. Keep a weather eye out in the West End and you never know your luck. In a way the obviousness of the pursuit almost undermines the glory.

Arguably more interesting are all the RMLs that *aren't* RML 2760. There you are, staring up at St Paul's, or sunning yourself in Trafalgar Square, or leaning over the railing at Marble Arch, and along comes an RML with an SMK registration; and irresistibly your eye is drawn to the second half of the number. It isn't... it can't be... can it possibly be *760F*? No it can't be, and it isn't. But you never know your luck.

Actually, the game has been slightly spoiled in recent years, because SMK 760F has been painted in a larger-than-life livery, and restored to something like its original condition. So it tends to stand out from the rest.

The irony is that on the rare occasions when I *have* photographed it, I've always done so more or less by chance. I was thinking of taking the picture anyway, and it just dawned on me at the last minute what bus I was looking at. The one time I was nearly caught out was in Fleet Street in 1988. I happened to turn, and there it was, almost too close to shoot; and in my excitement I nearly stepped in front of a taxi emerging from a side street.

The last RML, and how to lose your cool.

... and only

FRM1 is the Routemaster that never was, or never became anything more: the proposed rear-engined successor to the famous front-engined fleet. By the time the prototype was developed in the mid-1960s, power politics in the Leyland group (of which its developer, AEC, was a member) had already virtually written the project off as a blind alley with no future. Existing Leyland bus models were considered adequate, so the prototype remained unique.

After public service on various routes, it was finally shifted to the outer reaches of Potters Bar, way beyond north London, where it was able to plod around on a service that required just one bus.

Twice during the 1970s I made a pilgrimage there from my home at that time, south of the river. The first time, marvel of marvels, I found FRM1 at the bus station; but astonishingly, I hadn't yet decided my destiny was to be a bus photographer. So I simply *looked* at it, noting some unsightly damage to the upper front area – and left *empty-handed*. Can you believe it? When I came to my senses and returned some months later with a camera, there was of course no sign of it. And that seemed to be that.

Then some years afterwards it was placed on the Round London Sightseeing Tour. Here was a last chance to photograph it in what passed for public service. Yet for months, it seemed, I would merely catch glimpses of it disappearing in the distance. One day I actually came up behind it in my car, and promptly followed it for several miles through Knightsbridge and Kensington, hoping for a chance to leap out and photograph it. No such luck.

Then one day I happened to be at Victoria – ostensibly on some other errand, but prudently carrying my camera – and there it was, meekly waiting for travellers to board. I strolled up, took a couple of shots, and off it went.

FRM1 in service? Surely any enthusiast worth the name has a picture of that.

1988: Ensign RT

Survived

It's remarkable how much the bus scene can change. Back in the late 1980s, Ensignbus was still a substantial operator of London Transport tendered services. If you went to Romford, deep in the heartland of its operating area, it had so many routes that it looked like some mysteriously undiscovered municipal operator. Its striking blue and silver livery always seemed immaculate.

Then it sold that operation to Hong Kong Citybus, whose yellow livery became as familiar as the blue had been. Capital Citybus, as it became, in turn joined FirstGroup, and yellow turned to red. Yet Ensign proved to have remarkable staying power, and later returned to the bus scene, complete with its original blue livery.

The glory days in Romford have passed now, but back in its heyday I went there one Saturday in 1988 to record what the Ensign fleet looked like at the time; and in the back of my mind was an awareness that the company was operating a couple of ex-London Transport RTs. But I had no idea what routes they were on or what frequencies they might be running at (if they were running

at all). In fact, after an hour of photographing an assortment of Bristol VRs, Metrobuses, Fleetlines and other gems, I'd forgotten the RTs were even on the agenda.

Then suddenly there was one of them, in full livery and running on a regular service. I couldn't believe my luck. A quick sprint clear of the bus stands, hoping the driver would stay clear of the kerb (and the long shadows cast by those hoardings), and there was the picture in the can.

Exactly what I had planned all along.

Revived

London Transport was thinking of refurbishing its long-wheelbase Routemasters. The word gradually seeped out as the 1990s dawned, and set off a wave of excitement in the bus world. This meant, surely, that Routemasters would last a good few years longer.

First came the re-engining programme, in which the original AEC units were replaced by new ones from Cummins and Iveco. That in itself more or less

Above left:
1994: Three-axle Olympian

Left:
1991: The Routemaster lives on

Above:
1989: Show buses, 1: the PR100 at the NEC

guaranteed the vehicles a new lease of life. But it was the body rebuilds that really clinched the rejuvenation. Stripping and repanelling banished years of paint on paint; new fluorescent interior lights supplanted the old tungsten bulbs (they were not universally liked, it should be said, but they did brighten up the interior); new moulded-plastic front domes replaced the scraped and dented panel-beaten originals.

I'd read there were one or two prototype conversions out and about in service, but I hadn't the slightest idea where to look for them. Then one day in August 1991 I was hovering at Victoria with my camera, when I suddenly became aware of a Routemaster in the London General fleet that was somehow larger than life: more brightly painted than its contemporaries, less lined with age – and crucially (at the time), bereft by design of its standard radiator badge.

The legend on the side said it all really – 'Refurbished by VL Midlands Service Centre & Yeates Bus & Coach'. Remember VL? Volvo Leyland? A short-lived sop to the traditionalists who resented Leyland for selling out to its Swedish arch-rival. Anyway, the point was made. I pressed the shutter. The future starts here.

Extended

How far is it legitimate to impose one's need to take pictures of buses on unsuspecting colleagues? One day in November 1994 I found myself unexpectedly putting that question to the test. I was in south Cumbria, photographing a lorry belonging to a well-known Barrow haulier called T. Brady & Son. The company's fleet engineer, a willing and enthusiastic man called Chris, was driving us to look at a couple of possible backdrops between Barrow and Ulverston, when suddenly one of the Stagecoach group's three-axle Olympian double-deckers came into view.

For those who may have forgotten, these remarkable buses date back to 1987, when Leyland was still Leyland and Stagecoach was in expansive mood. Having ordered 30 conventional two-axle Olympians, it added a trio of

Left:
1997: Show buses, 2: the same PR100 in Scunthorpe

Below:
1989: Show buses, 3: Dart G349 GCK at the NEC

Right:
1997: Show buses, 4: Dart G350 GCK in King's Lynn

three-axle models based on Leyland's existing Hong Kong specification, the idea being to test their viability in UK markets.

'I want to photograph that bus,' I blurted out. 'Can you stop?'

You've got to give the man from Brady's his due. He may have flashed me a wild look, but he immediately swung over and on to the verge. I jumped out, and thankfully the bus pulled in at a bus stop almost opposite. I got the picture, the bus pulled away, and I like to think I kept most of my composure as I climbed back into the car.

You'd have to ask the man from Brady's what he really thought.

Rejected

I don't often photograph buses in Scunthorpe, although I don't really know why not. As a town it's unfairly maligned, and it does have its share of interesting vehicles. I suppose it's a long way from London, so I'm seldom within reach.

I was there one sunny summer's day in 1997 for possibly the second time in my life, photographing whatever buses chanced to pass. I had no special expectations – mainly the hope of seeing a few Road Car buses before hurrying on to Grimsby. Suddenly something unexpected materialised: a full-sized Renault single-decker in the livery of Hornsby Travel. Surely this had to be the prototype PR100 delivered to London Transport, and passed on when London decided it wasn't

suitable and Renault seemed to lose interest? It slowed to turn at the crossroads where I was standing, and I got the shot.

Later on the same trip, I found myself much further down the coast at King's Lynn. Here I'd been more often, although not with much more to show for it. Bus activity always seems strangely muted, and tends to revolve round the bus station. Inevitably, that was where I ended up this time. And, lo and behold, could this be another prototype – a Carlyle-bodied Dennis Dart in the livery of Norfolk Green?

I'll be truthful; I wasn't sure. But when I looked it up later, I found it was consecutively registered after the one I'd photographed in London livery on the Dennis stand at the Coach & Bus show in 1989. And remarkably, the PR100 in Scunthorpe had appeared on the Renault stand at the self-same show – also in London livery, and bearing an NC badge to identify Northern Counties as the builder of the Renault-style body.

Coincidence? No such thing in this business.

Remodelled

It's hard to imagine a time when Nottingham wasn't a magnet for those who prize the offbeat. Where else would you find a municipal operator that was still specifying its own unique body styles right into the 1980s? Even when it became reconciled to more conventional designs, it kept up the interest by buying demonstrators, short-run models and first batches of new chassis types. And it tended to rebuild, remould and reinvent what it already had.

9

For years I wanted to catch a certain T-registration Atlantean that had benefited from a rather radical front treatment; but when your time is limited, your expectations of finding a specific vehicle can't be too high. When I found myself there in June of 1996, my objective was elsewhere: to photograph one of the batch of four Dennis Arrows with Northern Counties Palatine II bodies that had just gone into service.

No problem; they were running on a route terminating deep in the city centre, so I could choose my shots with care. Then I wandered up to the main road near the theatre, leaning over the railings and watching Trent buses sweep past. And suddenly, there was the unique Atlantean, with its angular Northern Counties body looking a lot more severe than any others of its breed. I caught it in mid-turn, marvelling.

I still marvel when I look at the photograph now.

I knew that
And then there are the pictures you take completely by chance – the ones you may not even recognise as having much value until someone else tips you the wink. Then you can imagine how the punters on *Antiques Roadshow* must feel – stunned as an expert reveals some unsuspected gem.

Must I give chapter and verse? The occasions are too numerous. Take one from 1997. I was in Sheffield, photographing the comings and goings of Mainline and Andrews buses, plus anything else of interest that came along. The shadows were lengthening, and nothing very

outstanding was coming into view. Then, as I waited for an interesting vehicle, a P-registration Alexander Y-type bus trundled past, bearing the red livery of a small independent called Thompson Travel. I took a perfunctory photograph and thought little of it. Another of the Scottish Bus Group's cast-off Leopards, I vaguely assumed.

Only later, as a more knowledgeable friend leafed through my collection, did I realise this was actually ex-Lothian, just a bit more unusual and interesting.

Of course it was. I knew that.

Below:
1996: Nottingham Atlantean

Bottom:
1997: Not a Scottish Bus Group Leopard.

GORGEOUS GAS
OR JUST HOT AIR?

Diesel has reigned supreme as the power source for buses since the early 1930s. However, there have always been challenges to its success. Alan Millar looks at the world of alternative fuels.

L et me take you back to the evening of 30 November 1999. A Tuesday. And let me take you into central London. You have a choice of destinations. Enter the hallowed portals of the Institution of Civil Engineers, within a few hundred yards of the Palace of Westminster and London Transport's headquarters, and you'll find a seminar addressing issues of the bus world in the gentlemanly and gentlewomanly manner you might expect of such an august institution. Alternatively, the atmosphere around Euston station — a couple of miles away — could hardly be more different, as riot police and eco-warrior anarchists face one another and train services are suspended for several hours.

The rioters are protesting against global free trade and many of the trappings of modern life, including the exploitation of oil reserves around the planet. The seminar hears, among other things, of a project by FirstGroup, Wright's and a few other players to develop a zero-emission British fuel-cell bus for the new century. The bus isn't intended to answer the rioters' protests, but its development is a sign of how anxious the automotive industry is to address widespread public concerns about the environment. It's also yet another in a long and none-too-successful line of alternative-fuel buses — gas and electric — to challenge the mighty diesel, particularly over the past 30 years.

By far the most prolific alternative-fuel bus was the trolleybus, developed in Germany around the same time as the first internal combustion-engined vehicles were appearing and which enjoyed a brief period of widespread British use, between the early 1930s and the late 1950s. To begin with, it was seen more as an alternative to the tram — an easily-driven electric vehicle that didn't require the expense of its own private tracks and which, as turn-of-the-century tracks and tramcars began to wear out, allowed local authorities, London Transport and a few private operators to retain their own electricity-generating and distribution equipment while gaining many of the benefits of buses.

In the 1930s, the trolleybus also offered two distinct advantages over the diesel or petrol bus. The great Depression drove coal prices to an all-time low, so electricity was artificially cheap, and home-produced fuel became increasingly attractive as World War 2 approached and oil imports were threatened by attacks on Allied shipping. Postwar, those advantages disappeared and so, by 1972, did the British trolleybus. It has yet to return.

One alternative to the diesel which has been abandoned in Britain is the trolleybus. Glasgow Corporation operated a fleet which included modern Crossley-bodied BUTs, destined to see less than 10 years' service. Critics of trolleybuses argue that they only move pollution from the street to the power-station. Stewart J. Brown

Similar motives prompted a rash of gas-bus developments around the same time. Birmingham, Rotherham, Lincoln, Chesterfield and Wallasey Corporations, together with Northern General Transport, all adapted petrol-bus engines to run on town gas. They were heavy, limited in range and, as highly unusual vehicles in otherwise largely standardised fleets, probably created more difficulties than they were likely to solve.

Then there was producer gas, created by burning a range of low-grade fuels like coal, wood or turf in a furnace on the vehicle itself. Towards the end of the 1930s, France and Italy led the way with this technology, but, while the British Government was happy to encourage tram operators to buy trolleybuses, there wasn't the same top-level enthusiasm for producer gas. Its most vigorous supporter was a company called High Speed Gas (Great Britain) Ltd which bought the old Gilford factory in West London and built two producer-gas buses, one based on a Gilford CF176, the other on a chassis from Sentinel which also built a handful of gas-powered lorries for HSG.

The Gilford-HSG's most publicised outings were in Scotland. Highland Transport, whose chairman saw a profit opportunity in selling producer-gas equipment in

Britain and ordered a French system for one of the company's Albions, bought the bus and claimed its fuel costs were only two-thirds of those for diesel buses and just a third of those for petrol ones. But it ran on relatively flat roads in open country, and Highland had a vested interest in persuading operators to run gas buses. When the same bus ran with Glasgow Corporation for 23 days during the 1938 Empire Exhibition, it was far less successful; this operator complained of its sluggish performance and unsuitability for city work.

Imagine that same operator's deep joy after war broke out and the Government decreed that a proportion of Britain's national bus fleet should run on producer gas. The operators following this programme, mostly using burners on separate trailers, were brave and honourable, but the results seem to have been as disappointing as Glasgow's experience of 1938; few ran anywhere after 1943 and — just as World War 1 town-gas buses were a short-lived interlude — there was no long-term killing to be made from selling this system in Britain.

So it was that the diesel bus reigned supreme from 1945, but interest in alternative fuels began to surface in the late 1960s, especially when the seemingly-secure Middle East fuel supplies came under threat. The 1956 Suez crisis had led to temporary fuel-rationing, but the issue came more sharply into focus 11 years later when the Six-Day War prompted Arab boycotts of Israel's western allies. Matters got worse in 1973 when the Yom Kippur War led the oil producers to ration supplies and drive up their prices. The same thing happened six years later with the Islamic Revolution in Iran. And all this coincided with growing concern about atmospheric pollution.

Ironically, just as Bradford's last trolleybuses were withdrawn in 1972 (hastened out of daily service by power-cuts and a miners' strike), a Government-funded trial of battery-electric minibuses began. The Department of Trade & Industry had two Willowbrook-bodied 17-seaters, with standing space for nine, built on Leyland 900FG truck chassis adapted using technology proven on milk-floats. They did the rounds with operators, including Leeds and Edinburgh Corporations, SELNEC PTE and the National Bus Company's Eastern Counties.

The battery-electric buses suffered from a handicap no one has yet satisfactorily overcome: they were too heavy and couldn't travel very far without needing to have their batteries recharged. Unladen, they weighed nearly eight tonnes, which is as heavy as a 53-seat Leyland Leopard; on city centre stop/start work, they could last about 35 miles between charges. While they were about as big as a battery-electric bus dared get in 1972, few operators had yet identified a viable role for a 26-passenger minibus of any sort, let alone one which spent longer being refuelled than carrying passengers.

SELNEC, Greater Manchester's innovative public transport provider, worked on its own ideas for something a tad more practical. These emerged late in 1973 in the Silent Rider, a battery-powered version of a 10m Seddon Pennine RU. For almost £100,000 including development costs, the Silent Rider offered some improvements over the DTI minibuses as it had two doors, seats for 43 passengers, and a range of 45 miles between 3½-hour charges. It was still desperately heavy, and indeed its 13-tonne unladen weight has never been exceeded by any bus operated since in Greater Manchester.

The theory — and it's notable that FirstGroup is propounding exactly the same one for its fuel-cell bus, nearly 30 years later — was that zero-emission battery buses could provide the additional peak-only journeys and spend the hours in-between with their batteries hooked up to a charger. But in the battle between costs and environment, there was no realistic contest. Low-volume, production Silent Riders were going to cost four times as much to buy as far more operationally-adaptable diesel double-deckers, even if fuel prices were rising. So this one-off prototype remained just that and saw only limited use.

But Greater Manchester Transport, as SELNEC had become, wasn't one to give up easily, and in 1975 added a 19-seat battery-electric Seddon midibus to its experimental fleet, for trials on Manchester's Centreline inter-station route. It managed a non-stop 86-mile proving run from Manchester to Birmingham at an average speed of 30mph; top speed was said to be 45mph and it was supposed to be able to run all day without recharging. But lead-acid battery technology meant this was still a frighteningly heavy machine, tipping the scales at around the same weight as the DTI minibuses, while diesel Seddon midis weighed around 4.5 tonnes unladen.

Towards the end of 1974, NBC entered the fray with a 10.3m Leyland National converted to battery traction. Rather than fit the batteries in the vehicle itself, which wasn't so easy on a relatively low-floor vehicle like the National, seven tonnes of them were towed behind on a two-axle trailer. Even so, with a 39mph maximum speed and acceptable hill-climbing capacity, it still only had a range of 50 miles when fully laden. In addition, the trailer took the bus over the maximum permitted vehicle-length of the day, so its limited operation was confined to Crosville duties on the private tracks of the Runcorn busway.

Thus it was that, apart from a 1979 electric Dodge 18-seater with Bournemouth, battery buses faded quietly from the British scene. Frequently, the Great and the Good of the bus industry attended conferences where the Great and the Good of the electric-vehicle industry told them that a revolution in battery technology was imminent and that unladen weight would fall as dramatically as range would increase.

Far left:
Battery power has, according to its proponents, always been on the verge of a breakthrough. Yet in terms of excessive weight and limited range, little has really changed since this demonstrator was tried three decades ago by the SELNEC PTE. Alan Millar collection

Top:
SELNEC and its successor, Greater Manchester, persevered with battery buses, and for a short while ran this Seddon midi — or so Lucas would have us believe. The heavy and obvious retouching of the picture suggests that the photographer made do with a diesel-powered bus which was doctored to become Greater Manchester's EX62. Alan Millar collection

Above:
EX62 being charged up. Let's hope they had plenty of 50-pence pieces for the electricity meter... Alan Millar collection

Left:
Are battery buses destined to be quaint runabouts? They come no more quaint than the Italian examples running for FirstGroup. This is a Technobus Gulliver which carries just nine people and weighs over four tonnes. Stewart J. Brown

Towards the end of 1993, the electric-vehicle people were able to show how far British battery-bus technology had really advanced when four electric Optare MetroRiders went into city-centre service with the Oxford Bus Company. And the answer? About 5 miles and ¾ of a tonne. This was a 7-tonne, 18-passenger bus with a 40mph top speed and a range of 55 miles. To be fair, the range was extendable by being able to plug the batteries into a power source between journeys, but a 4.4-tonne diesel MetroRider could carry 40 passengers, didn't take 12 hours to be recharged and ran for 300 miles on a full tank of diesel.

There was a potentially more promising alternative from Italy: the hybrid bus. Iveco had done some encouraging work on small buses for congested, historic city centres in its home country, and persuaded Transit Holdings to take a couple of adapted DailyBus midibuses for trials in Exeter. These vehicles, costing £100,000 apiece, each carried 4 tonnes of lead-acid batteries which were charged by the 997cc petrol engine from the Fiat Uno car; for most of the day, they ran with the engine and electric motor running, but the engine could be switched off for 20 minutes of each hour for zero-emission city-centre running. They ran for less than a year before being taken out of service with a view to fitting new-technology nickel-hydride batteries, which were supposed to be half the weight of the lead-acid units and capable of charging more reliably. There was also talk of Transit running Neoplan nickel-hydride hybrids in Portsmouth, but Transit sold its British bus operations before any of this came to pass, and neither Stagecoach (which inherited the Exeter buses and, thanks to a contract change, the equally troubled Oxford MetroRiders) nor FirstGroup (which bought the Portsmouth business) was minded to pursue these particular initiatives. But FirstGroup did have its own hybrid project to work on in Portsmouth. Thanks to the same European Union project which would have funded Transit's Neoplans, it spent £110,000 converting a nine-year-old Mercedes-Benz 609D 25-seater into a 20-seater with capability of running in electric, diesel or diesel-electric mode. Hybrid propulsion kept unladen weight down — and we're talking relatively, for pure diesels are still much lighter — to 5.2 tonnes, but its range was limited and FirstGroup tried not running after dark when its lights would drain battery power.

The same group also became involved in pure battery bus operation in 1998 when eight left-hand-drive Technobus Gulliver midis were imported from Italy for operation in Bristol and Birkenhead. This was another design created originally for mediæval Italian city centres, and in British operation it was hamstrung by some rather over-zealous domestic interpretation of rules which prevent standing passengers being carried in buses with

There's nothing new about gas-powered buses. A Teesside Municipal Transport Fleetline was fitted with a Rolls-Royce engine in 1973 and was promoted as the 'clean-air bus'. Stewart J. Brown collection

fewer than 14 seats; FirstGroup's Gullivers ran with just nine seats, eight of them in facing rows separated by what, in the circumstances, was an absurdly wide doorway. Thanks to its glassfibre body, the Gulliver weighed in at 4 tonnes unladen, and battery-range was around 60 miles; top speed, on the other hand, was a less-than-inspiring 20mph, which may be fine in historic city centres, but hardly sparkled in Bristol or Birkenhead.

And then there was the sad tale of Strathclyde PTE's electric Omnis. Although it had lost its bus operations back in 1986, like other PTEs it never quite lost the urge to do some of the things that bus operators do, and in 1996 it placed an order for three low-floor, six-wheel, battery-powered Omni midibuses for the tendered service linking Glasgow's main-line railway stations and Buchanan bus station. As a city-centre operation, it made some sense for it to be a zero-emission route.

The first complication was the collapse of Omni soon after the order was placed, but the buses were built and delivered around the beginning of 1998. However, a greater obstacle was that the section of route between Queen Street railway station and Buchanan bus station is uphill, and hills drain batteries. It transpired that any operator tendering to run the Omnis would need to charge its PTE client a lot more than if it used low-emission diesels. That's why the three buses were still sitting unused in February 2000 as this story was being written, and why they are the most visible evidence of how little progress battery-electric buses have made in Britain in 28 years of optimistic trials.

The revival of British gas-bus operation has gained a shade more momentum in recent years, but has still to progress beyond the experimental stage.

It started in 1973, when — with Department of the Environment encouragement — Teesside Municipal Transport replaced the Gardner 6LW engine in a Daimler Fleetline with a very compact, eight-cylinder Rolls-Royce B81G industrial engine fuelled by liquefied petroleum gas — a by-product of oil production. The work was carried out in partnership with Calor Gas, which then, as much more recently, spotted an opportunity to sell public transport operators the virtues of a much cleaner fuel which also happens to make for a much quieter-running engine.

There were drawbacks, not the least of which was the extra strength which had to be built into the bus's fuel tank to reduce the risk of dangerous gas leaks; and as the B81G was an adapted petrol engine, it reintroduced the bus industry to the forgotten art of maintaining spark-plugs. Teesside became Cleveland Transit and kept the Fleetline running for four years, during which time it clocked up over 100,000 miles. In 1979, a similar engine went into a South Yorkshire PTE Leyland Atlantean, and 1980 saw NBC fitting an LPG version of Leyland's 680 in a Ribble Atlantean.

The results were hardly encouraging. The Cleveland Fleetline's fuel consumption of 3.4mpg compared poorly with the diesel Gardner, and Ribble claimed its Atlantean was 58% more expensive per mile on fuel than otherwise identical diesels.

Like battery buses, gas ones faded out of the picture as the industry faced the more pressing concerns of the loss of Bus Grant, and the approach of deregulation and privatisation, but there always are optimists abroad who will push their bright ideas. And so it was with gas buses, especially as vehicles powered by compressed natural gas (CNG) were beginning to establish a foothold in parts of Europe and North America, and both vehicle manufacturers and gas suppliers were waking up to a business opportunity.

Southampton Citybus bought 10 new Dennis Darts with Cummins CNG engines. They were refuelled overnight from a mains gas supply. The gas was stored in tanks on the roof, concealed under a glass-fibre fairing. Plaxton

Their enthusiasm was also being driven by the relentless pace of emissions legislation in both continents, and the need for diesel engines to be substantially redesigned roughly every five years to comply with new standards. If this level of investment was reflected in significantly more expensive diesel engines, then volume-produced gas engines might not be quite so forbiddingly expensive after all. And there also appeared to be growing evidence of serious health risks associated with the tiny particles in diesel exhaust.

It was 1993 when all these thoughts began to be turned into action and what may at first have seemed an unlikely operator converted an equally unlikely bus to run on LPG. The operator was Guide Friday, the open-top tour-bus company, and the bus (the first of several conversions) was an 18-year-old Atlantean which quite likely cost as much to have its 250,000-mile 680 engine converted to LPG as it had to buy from Nottingham some years earlier, but Guide Friday had two good reasons for using LPG. One was its interest in a Danish-based

company offering similar conversions to other operators; the other was that its buses ran through sensitive historic centres where their presence wasn't universally appreciated, so anything that made these green-painted buses environmentally green could only be a step in the right direction — even if fuel consumption was as poor as in the Ribble and Cleveland experiments.

Later the same year, the Department of Transport came up with £100,000 in grants towards trials of both LPG and CNG buses. Reading Buses got the UK's first CNG-fuelled bus, a MetroRider, during 1994. It was powered by an adapted Rover V8 petrol engine in place of the standard Cummins B-series, although Cummins was already producing CNG engines in the United States. Southampton Citybus converted six Carlyle-bodied Dennis Darts to CNG, using their original B-series engines. At the same time, Badgerline — destined soon to become part of FirstGroup — took advantage of Guide Friday's expertise to have a pair of 18-year-old Gardner-engined Bristol VRs converted to run on LPG.

This looked like the start of something big, as FirstGroup entered 1996 with the first brand new CNG-fuelled Dart (in Bristol), and Southampton Citybus — soon to be acquired by FirstGroup and cashing in on European grants — bought 10 similar vehicles, while Cambus ordered two Cummins CNG-fuelled MetroRiders for a Cambridge city-centre service. By 1997, FirstGroup was further on to the alternative-fuel bandwagon with an order for seven CNG-fuelled Volvo B10Ls with Alexander Ultra bodies for Northampton; Travel West Midlands promptly trumped that by taking twice as many similar Volvos for a route in Walsall.

The LPG option was pushed by the one vehicle manufacturer with the technology at its fingertips and the one bus-operating group with an interest in selling that manufacturer's products. The manufacturer was DAF, which had developed production LPG engines on the back of plentiful LPG supplies in its native Netherlands, and the group was Arriva, which imported DAF buses and coaches for all to buy or rent.

Two Plaxton-bodied, LPG-fuelled SB220 low-floor demonstrators were built to show the potential for a fuel which is less awkward to handle than CNG and is used more widely in Europe. Arriva worked hard, along with Calor and Shell, at persuading operators and local authorities of the advantages of running these buses, and succeeded in putting one bus into a FirstGroup fleet — Crosville, for park-and-ride routes in Chester. But its best successes were with Arriva fleets which, at the time of writing, had taken 17 for routes in Chester, Glasgow and Watford; Go-Ahead's London Central got three LPG-fuelled SB220s late in 1999 as part of the East Lancs-bodied Millennium Transit fleet operated to the Greenwich Dome.

It's progress, but hardly indicative of building up of a head of steam in favour of gas buses, which remain more expensive to operate than diesels, even if they are cleaner and quieter, and which require separate fuelling, storage and maintenance systems to support them.

And that is where the fuel-cell bus might come in. It's called Futurbus, which is a horribly contrived acronym — 'Fu' for Fuel-cell, 't' for technology, 'ur' for urban and 'bus' for, well, bus. The plan is that it should be undergoing off-road trials around the time this book goes on sale, and that a pre-production version could be around three years later.

Because of the complications experienced with its gas buses, FirstGroup wants this vehicle to run on conventional diesel, although the prototype will have an adapted petrol engine. The design brief is for it to be capable of a 55mph maximum speed and a 250-mile range, and of being recharged in seven minutes, rather than several hours as happens with battery buses. And,

Left:
DAF has supplied LPG-powered buses to a number of UK fleets, including Arriva Cymru. This one is running on a park-and-ride service in Chester and has Plaxton Prestige bodywork. Arriva Bus & Coach

Inset:
Badgerline operated a 'Clean Fuel Bus' in Bath in the late 1990s, with the unlikely marriage of 1960s technology (Bristol VRT) and 1990s eco-friendly fuel (LPG). Stewart J. Brown

Below:
Guide Friday, operating in historic Stratford, promotes the benefits of LPG on the sides of its buses. Stewart J. Brown

in case you were wondering, a fuel-cell vehicle essentially carries its own little mobile power-station, using a variety of fuels to generate the electricity needed to power its traction-motors. It thus does away with the seemingly insuperable weight penalty of lead-acid batteries.

The British vehicle won't be the first in the world, for there are prototypes in North America and Germany, where various fuels like methanol and hydrogen have been tried, but it is the first to be commissioned by a commercial bus company. Not that it will be cheap, for new technology often comes at a forbidding price before volume production can be contemplated, and it's by no means guaranteed that Futurbus will ever be financially viable.

And the trolleybus? It's still alive and well in pockets around the world. Indeed, as I write this, the polluted cities of Athens and San Francisco are both investing in new trolleybuses, even in route extensions, but fate has prevented a British comeback so far. For some years, West Yorkshire PTE planned to reintroduce them in Bradford, which was one of Britain's first trolleybus towns as well as its last, but those schemes lost out to electrified railways and guided diesel buses.

More recently, there was an ambitious plan for an electronically-guided rapid-transit line in Liverpool which was to use what the promoters called 'rubber-tyred transit vehicles', but which those of us old enough or sufficiently widely-travelled to know otherwise chose to call articulated trolleybuses. The scheme was thrown out by the Government, but there is a chance that a similar line might be created around the Greenwich and Woolwich areas of southeast London after the Millennium Dome is closed.

For the time being, though, there seems little reason to doubt that most buses will continue to be fuelled by diesel, but 30 years of development must surely, some day, bear fruit in the shape of a practical alternative. Otherwise all the research and testing of prototypes will have been nothing but a huge waste of effort.

San Francisco's trolleybus fleet has since the late 1970s comprised 343 Canadian-built Flyers. New trolleybuses are on order. Stewart J. Brown

A CENTURY
OF MANCHESTER'S
BUSES

Reg Wilson takes a brief look at
Manchester's buses in the 20th century.

Manchester's experience was in many ways typical of the changes in public transport provision seen in most cities in the UK during the 20th century. But it had the added complexity of having not only horsebuses, horse trams, electric trams, petrol and diesel buses, trolleybuses and experimental electric buses, but also of undergoing the PTE experience, welcoming a resurgence of the tramway and ending up with its major bus operations controlled by not one — as in other conurbations — but two of the greatest post-deregulation groups. Featuring only the bus side of these changes is more than enough for one compact article, even when restricting coverage to Manchester municipal vehicles and those of its post-1969 successors.

The century opened with the Manchester Carriage & Tramways Co, successor to John Greenwood's 1824 service, operating horsebuses to supplement and feed the horse tramway routes. When the leases terminated, Manchester Corporation Tramways Department, established in 1901, gradually took over the company's activities within its own boundaries and those of several smaller neighbouring authorities. It opened its first electric tram route on 6 June 1901, and the final company horse tram working was on 31 March 1903. Horsebus services continued under MCTD ownership in areas not served by rail.

Manchester's first motorbus was a Critchley-Norris, borrowed for a trial in 1904 but not purchased. However, competition from the short-lived Manchester District Motor Omnibus Co in 1906 led to the Corporation acquiring three Leylands with Crossley engines to take over horsebus services

beyond the tram terminus at West Didsbury. Complaints from residents led to a two-year reinstatement of horse power, but by the end of 1908 motorised vehicles had become more generally accepted. Around that time trolleybuses, then in an early stage of development, were considered but rejected.

Horsebuses appeared occasionally as substitutes until 1915, and even after that saw some outlying service. (A splendid example of a company-owned horsebus which was later operated by the Corporation can be seen at the Greater Manchester Museum of Transport.) By 1924 the motorbus fleet topped 30 vehicles; 10 years later, when the tram was beginning to slide into second place, a tenfold increase had occurred and diesel engines were becoming the norm.

In the years that followed, Manchester Corporation introduced trolleybuses, which ran for a little over a quarter of a century, and abandoned its trams. Rear-engined buses were adopted, slowly at first, and culminated in the striking Mancunian. The Corporation then gave way to the newly-created Passenger Transport Executive in 1969. Deregulation in 1986 saw the start of a process which led, at the close of the 20th century, to the city's main services being provided by Stagecoach and FirstGroup.

Highlights of the unfolding story are told in the extended captions which follow.

Right:
One of the 3hp buses taken over by the Corporation from the Manchester Carriage & Tramways Co during 1901-3 stands at the Church Inn, Northenden, outer terminus of a route started in 1902 which connected with the tramway at West Didsbury. Above the bus the Cyclists Touring Club badge is fixed to the pub wall — a frequent adornment on rural hostelries at that time. Manchester's coat of arms had replaced the MC&T title and the conductor — or guard, in Manchester parlance — wears a style of uniform which lasted until after World War 2.
Courtesy Chris Heaps

Posed against the same pub as the horsebus is No 3, one of the three Leylands with Crossley engines which in July 1906 became the first mechanically-propelled Corporation-owned buses to enter service in Manchester. The body was by Dick, Kerr of Preston and seated 33. In 1909 this bus was converted to a tower-wagon for maintenance of the tramway overhead. courtesy Chris Heaps

By 1928 bus design had progressed to a point where single-deckers — always a minority in the Manchester fleet — were visually the ancestors of today's models. The skirts were deeper and the floor was lower, windows were no longer tram-like, and pneumatic tyres were universal. This is one of five Crossley Eagles which entered service in January 1929. The bodies were 32-seaters by Dodson and the type, with manager R. Stuart Pilcher's Edinburgh-style cutaway rear entrance, became the Department's standard layout for a decade. courtesy Chris Heaps

In 1927 Manchester bought six of the few Bristol A double-deckers to be built, and in the same year Leyland's Titan TD1 demonstrator appeared. In appearance these designs were a generation apart, and the Bristols were the last Manchester buses to show tramcar influence in their styling. They are all shown in this manufacturer's photograph and were relatively successful, lasting until 1935. The open-staired Bristol bodies seated 52 and power came from a four-cylinder Bristol engine, petrol-driven of course at this stage in the development of the motorbus. Reg Wilson collection

Above:
The Leyland Titan was dramatically different from previous double-deck types. The so-called 'piano-front' style of body, introduced by Leyland on its 1927 Titan prototype, was imitated by other builders. Manchester 225, the first of 12 delivered in February 1930, had a 50-seat body built by Short Bros at the company's seaplane factory in Rochester, Kent. Fitted with a new MCTD/Crossley body in 1935, this TD1 survived until 1949. Short Bros

Left:
Manchester did not permit external bus advertising until after 1948, so this streamlined livery reigned unspoilt for 10 years. Most buses wore this version, seen on one of the Corporation's first trolleybuses, a Crossley TDD4 new in March 1938 with Crossley/Metro-Cammell body. No original 'piano-fronts' or earlier non-streamlined bodies received swoops retrospectively, but a few Crossley Condors and Leyland TD2s did so after virtual rebodying. Around 1942 grey replaced cream on many buses (but not trams or trolleybuses) due to wartime paint shortages; red/grey buses were still in service in the late 1940s. Trolleybus withdrawals commenced in the early 1950s, and this bus lasted until 1956. Crossley

Above:
Manchester's standard postwar body style continued the dipped front upstairs windows which had characterised deliveries from 1936 to 1941. Another design feature employed a cantilevered rear platform which required a strengthened upper frame. This was hidden by partial infills of the two rear top-deck windows, matched for visual balance by the same downstairs. The style was used on hundreds of Leyland and Daimler buses, and Crossley buses and trolleybuses, from 1946 to 1952. Some buses were 7ft 6in wide but after 1948 the norm became 8ft, permitted by new regulations. Depicted is an October 1946 Crossley DD42/3 with 7ft 6in-wide 56-seat Crossley body. This was one of the final batch to carry a lower-deck swoop when new, but by the time it was photographed in April 1955 that had long since vanished during a repaint. Despite problems with some Crossley engines (many of this batch were refitted with used Leyland units), 2938 provided 16 years of service. Reg Wilson

Most later PD2 deliveries carried 64-seat Metro-Cammell Orion bodies, a type almost standard for Manchester between 1953 and 1963. Route 1 to Gatley, then just outside the city boundary in Cheshire, ran with limited stopping places and was almost an express. This photograph dates from Christmas Eve 1956 when 3464 was three months old, and was taken on a loading bay between Piccadilly bus station and Moseley Street. Reg Wilson

The city's first rear-engined double-deckers were 10 Leyland Atlantean PDR1/1s which arrived in late 1959, a full five years before the last half-cab rear-loader was delivered. The Department was evidently being cautious. Confidence in rear engines boosted (and union opposition overcome), Daimler Fleetlines with 76-seat Metro-Cammell bodies were ordered in 1962/3 and 4625 of the second batch is seen in September 1964 in Piccadilly bus station. At that time registration authorities were very helpful in allocating long runs of numbers to match fleet numbers, in contrast to the position 30 years later when numbers thought to be potentially attractive are withheld in case the opportunity arises to sell them at a profit. Reg Wilson

Following the introduction of a brighter cream and red single-deck livery on Leyland Panthers in 1967, a white and red double-deck version was applied to Park Royal Mancunian bodies, the first double-deckers to be purpose-built for one-man-operation. Deliveries started in February 1968, with Leyland Atlanteans coming first, and on Saturday 24 February 1001 and 1024 were displayed in Piccadilly, with the latter giving short free rides, as seen here. With the last trolleybuses (numbered in the 1000s) and the last Crossleys (in the 2000s) having been withdrawn, a revision of fleet numbering blocks became possible, and Mancunian-style Fleetlines, delivered from June, started at 2001. The official entry into service of the Atlanteans, equipped with no-ticket Johnson fareboxes as denoted by the symbol above the windscreen, was on 1 April. The last Mancunians were delivered after SELNEC took over. Reg Wilson

In August 1972, nearly three years after the formation of SELNEC, there appeared the first of large orders for Atlanteans and Fleetlines with a new style of standard body built by Park Royal and Northern Counties. These were numbered in a single series — irrespective of chassis make — commencing at 7001, and the first of the new standards were registered in three batches by the Central, Northern and Southern Divisions of SELNEC. 7252, a Central Fleetline with Northern Counties body and Manchester registration, is seen in Portland Street in August 1973. Reg Wilson

In George Street — a location now occupied by Metrolink track — three GMT livery variants are seen on 14 January 1984. The MCW Metrobus carries a livery confined mainly to that type, and happens to be standing on the spot where Manchester's last tram made its final departure 35 years earlier, on 10 January 1949. To the left is a Northern Counties standard Fleetline, and on the right a Park Royal standard Atlantean in the brown, orange and white introduced by GMT in 1981. Reg Wilson

Right:

When GM Buses came into existence on 26 October 1986 only minor livery changes occurred. A lighter band of colour — which differentiated between areas — appeared on the lower panels with a new logo and local fleetname above the doors, all being added to the established brown, orange and white livery. 2011, seen leaving Stockport bus station in March 1987, is one of 30 Dennis Dominators with Northern Counties bodies delivered in the spring of 1985. *Reg Wilson*

Below:

Yet another change of livery followed soon after the creation of GM Buses — plain orange and white. Atlantean 8622 is seen leaving Liverpool for Wigan in May 1989. At that time GM Buses' vehicles were seen on Merseyside only once an hour, but a short-lived outbreak of fierce competition would see GM Buses running all over Merseyside — including the Wirral and Southport — in the mid-1990s. *Reg Wilson*

Left:

Following the split into GM Buses (North) and GM Buses (South), both operations modified the orange livery they had inherited. The GM Buses (South) approach, with 'GMS Buses' fleetname, is seen on 301, the first of a batch of Alexander-bodied Volvo B6s which had been hired from Stagecoach. This is a May 1995 view, taken just yards away from the spot where a terrorist bomb would create havoc in June 1996. Reg Wilson

Above:

By May 1996, only two months after being bought by FirstBus, a new overall orange livery — described as 'rail red' — appeared for GM Buses (North). A 1996 Volvo B6LE with Wright body, 1077, is seen in Oldham Street in May 1998.
Reg Wilson

Right:
During a period of indecision about liveries for premium services at GM Buses (North), many Dennis Dart SLFs with Plaxton Pointer 2 bodies entered service in late 1997 wearing an ivory livery with blue relief. A gold band on the cantrail emphasised 'Gold Service'. Until April 1998 the fleetname was 'Greater Manchester', accompanied by the FirstBus 'f' logo. 6039 is seen in Wigan in March 1998. This livery was short-lived. Reg Wilson

Below:
GM Buses (South) was bought by Stagecoach in January 1996 and rebranded 'Stagecoach Manchester' from 1 April. During 1996 Stagecoach corporate colours flooded south Manchester as the fleet was repainted and new buses arrived in quantity. Volvo B6LE 350 was one of a large batch delivered in the first quarter of 1997 and has a 36-seat Alexander ALX200 body; it is seen leaving Stockport bus station in May 1997. At the end of 1998 this bus was transferred to Midland Red South.
Reg Wilson

OWNERS OF MANCHESTER'S BUSES: A CHRONOLOGY

FROM	TO	OWNER
	to 1903	Manchester Carriage & Tramways Co
1 Apr 1901	31 Oct 1969	Manchester Corporation Transport Department
1 Nov 1969	31 Mar 1974	SELNEC PTA
1 Apr 1974	25 Oct 1986	Greater Manchester PTA
26 Oct 1986	12 Dec 1993	Greater Manchester Buses
13 Dec 1993	31 Mar 1994	GM Buses North and GM Buses South
1 Apr 1994		Management/employee buy-outs
29 Jan 1996		GMB(S) bought by Stagecoach; rebranded 'Stagecoach Manchest
7 Mar 1996		GMB(N) bought by FirstBus; renamed 'First Manchester' in 1999

THE *END* OF SMT

SMT, the initials of the Scottish Motor Traction Co, featured in Scotland's bus industry for a large part of the 20th century, finally being abandoned by the last user, FirstGroup, in 1999.
Billy Nicol illustrates SMT in the early 1990s.

Left:
The SMT logo was carried by a variety of different double-deck types, including Leyland Olympians, most bought new and with bodywork by ECW or, as here, Alexander. The livery was dark green and cream.

Below:
There were also Ailsas in the fleet. This Alexander-bodied bus was new to Western but reached SMT via Clydeside. It is seen in Edinburgh's famous Princes Street in 1993, with a later Ailsa behind.

THE *END* OF SMT

This picture:
The Alexander Y-type was one of the most common types of bus in Scotland for three decades. Most were on Leyland Leopard chassis, but Eastern Scottish (and Western SMT) had a number on Seddon Pennine VIIs. This SMT Seddon has the multi-windowed 53-seat bus variant of the Y-type body.

Above:
Not all 1990s Eastern Scottish vehicles carried the SMT name. Scottish Citylink livery is worn by a hired Van Hool-bodied DAF SB3000 operating on the Glasgow-Edinburgh express service.

Above:
After buying Dodge/Renault minibuses, Eastern Scottish switched to the Optare MetroRider, ordering two batches, in 1992 and 1994. One of the original delivery is seen in Edinburgh's St Andrew's Square, wearing the lighter green relief applied to new buses at that time.

Right:
The brighter livery was also used on older buses allocated to Diamond Service routes, where a higher standard of service was provided. These included this unusual bus, a Leyland Lion with Alexander body. The mid-engined Lion was Leyland's response to the Volvo Citybus, but found fewer buyers.

LATE
DEVELOPER

Gavin Booth, editor of Classic Bus and a life-long Leyland devotee, reviews the history of the Atlantean as the remaining examples in big fleets disappear rapidly.

Most of the bodywork on the first PDR1s looked like this regardless of the builder — in this case Roe. New to Devon General, this 1960 bus is seen in 1981 running for Western National, demonstrating that, whatever problems they may have had, early Atlanteans could be long-lived. *All photographs by the author*

Forget young-looking policemen. It's a sure sign that you're getting old when you have experienced the entire career of a type of bus. Especially when that career stretches over 40 years.

When I was a teenager in the 1950s, buses like the AEC Regent or Leyland Titan represented the ultimate development of designs that had been introduced 25 years earlier. So when Leyland introduced the rear-engined Atlantean in 1956, impressionable teenagers like myself were bowled over by its futuristic appearance. Overnight, Regents and Titans looked old-fashioned; even the Routemaster, arguably the most handsome front-engined double-decker ever, couldn't hold a light to the Atlantean — or so we thought, in our naïve teenage way.

At its most basic, there were strong similarities between the Titan PD3 and the Atlantean. Many of the components were common, but mounting the vertical O.600 9.8-litre engine transversely at the rear suddenly released a lot more space for passengers, and gave the driver direct control of the entrance door.

Passenger space was what it was all about in 1956 when the prototype Atlantean was revealed to a fairly gobsmacked world. Bus companies were still experiencing passenger loadings that were best dealt with by big buses. In a 27ft-long double-decker, 66 was the highest number of seated passengers, but in an Atlantean to the newly-relaxed 30ft length, 78 was possible. Admittedly, 74 was possible in a Leyland PD3 to the same length, but the shortcomings of the PD3 were laid bare in the 1960s when one-man double-deckers were legalised. Then the Atlantean came into its own, and the PD3 and its front-engined brothers were on the way out.

The Atlantean didn't just happen. Leyland had been experimenting with alternatives to the traditional front engine since the 1930s. In that decade it had built a prototype rear-engined single-deck bus, as well as 49 rear-engined Leyland Cubs for London Transport. And it had returned to the theme in 1952 with the first of two Lowloaders, double-deckers with Leyland's turbocharged O.350 engine mounted on the rear platform. In-service experience with the first of the Lowloaders prompted Leyland to refine the concept with the beefier O.600

engine, and the legalisation of 30ft double-deckers in 1956 suddenly gave the concept legs. At first, Leyland designed the Atlantean as an integral lowheight model, just 13ft 3in high, but after operators had inspected and operated the 1956 prototype, they made it clear to Leyland that they were looking for a separate chassis to be bodied by their favoured bodybuilders. Leyland would experience a similar response to the Titan B15 some 20 years later, hence the highly successful Olympian.

At the Atlantean's 1958 launch as a separate chassis, Leyland must have wished that it had the market to itself, but the truth is that Leyland's rivals — and it still had some when the Atlantean was launched — were quick to recognise the dangers it posed, and produced competing models. First was the Guy Wulfrunian, not rear-engined like the Atlantean, but front-engined with the Gardner 6LX squeezed on to the front platform between the driver and the entrance. The Wulfrunian, as we surely all know, was not a happy bus, and played its part in the fall of the once-proud Guy name. Guy passed to Jaguar in 1961, which the previous year had bought Daimler.

In 1960 Daimler had introduced the Fleetline, which was the real Atlantean challenger. Daimler had long been a major supplier of mainly municipal buses, but sales were flagging as the 1950s progressed. The Fleetline, Gardner-engined to please economy-conscious engineers, stole a march on the Atlantean by offering a true low-height capability. On production Atlanteans low overall height of 13ft 4in could only be achieved by four awkward rows of four-across lowbridge-type seats at the rear of the upper deck.

Leyland had the advantage of a head start on Daimler, and picked up some impressive orders when it went into production in 1958. The BET group was a good Atlantean customer from day one, and firms like Devon General, Northern General, Potteries and Ribble were early users. Many other operators held back to see how this revolutionary new model performed, and only started buying once the early bugs had been engineered out. Others, possibly knowing the Fleetline was on its way, held out for the Gardner-engined model; others still stuck doggedly to front-engined models.

There were just four double-deck builders of any importance in Britain at this time — two if you based it on sales. AEC and Leyland were way ahead of Daimler and Guy, and looked impregnable. Then everything changed.

We have seen that Daimler and Guy found themselves under Jaguar control, and in 1963 the unthinkable happened and AEC and Leyland 'merged'. AEC had not followed Leyland down the rear-engined route, and at the time of the merger offered the Regent V and Renown as its double-deck models. Leyland continued to offer the Titan, and Daimler and Guy also offered front-engined models, but fewer and fewer orders were coming in. The new Leyland Motor Corporation tolerated this internal competition for a few years, but quickly dropped the front-engined models at the end of the 1960s — hardly surprising when the new Bus Grant scheme offered a subsidy of 25% towards the cost of new buses suitable for driver-only operation.

Right:
Edinburgh City Transport and Lothian, its post-1975 successor, standardised on the Atlantean/Alexander combination; most were panoramic-windowed two-door buses. The last were withdrawn at the start of the new millennium.

Back to the early Atlanteans and the effect they had on this young enthusiast. Glasgow Corporation got Scotland's first Atlantean, and I know I was not the only enthusiast to make the pilgrimage to Glasgow early in 1959 to sample this revolutionary new bus. And I'm sure my contemporaries in other parts of Britain were beating a path to Ammanford, or Hastings, or Wallasey — or one of the other towns and cities where early Atlanteans could be found.

It would be wrong to pretend that the early Atlanteans were flawless. Although the model had been in development for a number of years before production started, manufacturers know to their cost that something that has been put together by the best engineering brains in the business, and driven endlessly round a test track, possibly subjected to extremes of temperature, falls apart when it is put into the hands of your average bus driver or mechanic. Every manufacturer has its own proving methods, and it must be tempting to follow the example of London Transport with the Routemaster, or Bristol with the Lodekka, and introduce prototypes for in-service testing before starting production. In the case of the Routemaster and Lodekka there was a five-year gap between first prototype and production, but these were models being developed for a known, captive market. Commercial pressures have meant that

some revolutionary models were put on to the market before they were quite ready. This seemed to be the case with the Atlantean, as operators found it was a rather more complex animal than the more familiar Titan PD2 or PD3. Part of the problem was probably a failure on the part of operators to adapt maintenance procedures to suit what was a very different bus. But some of the blame must rest with Leyland, which was still getting to grips with the eccentricities of rear-engined buses.

Above:
All of the major bodybuilders active in Britain built bodywork on the Atlantean. The least common came from Massey Bros of Wigan, which built small numbers — mainly for the municipal fleets of Maidstone and Colchester. A Colchester bus loads in the town's High Street.

CIE built up a big fleet of Atlanteans from 1966. Early vehicles had CIE's own distinctive bodywork, with buses delivered from 1968 being of two-door layout. The location is Dublin; the year, 1980.

Right:
Leeds City Transport standardised on 33ft-long double-deckers with two-door Roe bodies. It bought both Fleetlines and Atlanteans; this is an AN68/2.

Below:
A number of independents bought new Atlanteans, including Cunningham of Paisley. An Alexander-bodied AN68 is seen turning at the Renfrew Ferry terminus of Cunningham's route from Paisley.

Right:
Most new double-deckers for NBC in the 1970s were ECW-bodied Bristol VRTs. However, some fleets did receive Atlanteans, including London Country, and often in substantial quantities. The standard NBC body was provided by Park Royal and, later, by Roe. This is a 1974 view of a new Park Royal-bodied bus on a hire at Chessington.

The troublesome centrifugal clutch fitted to the original PDR1/1 Atlantean was abandoned in 1963 when the Mk II version appeared; this had an SCG fluid-friction clutch with a fluid flywheel for starting from rest and a centrifugal clutch which engaged at higher speeds. At the same time, a slightly more powerful version of the O.600 engine was fitted. In some cases operators specified the optional O.680 11.1-litre engine.

The success of the Daimler Fleetline was not going unnoticed at Leyland. Some important early customers for the awkward semi-lowbridge Atlantean had switched allegiance to the Fleetline, and by 1964 the Fleetline was actually outselling the Atlantean. One attempt to rescue the situation was the appearance of the true lowheight PDR1/2 model in 1964, with the drop-centre rear axle that had been developed for the Albion Lowlander, and the same Daimler gearbox as fitted to the Fleetline. The longer-wheelbase PDR2/1 model appeared in 1966, suitable for 33ft bodywork, and the lowheight PDR1/2 was replaced in 1967 by the PDR1/3, with a return to the Pneumocyclic gearbox.

Although Leyland lost some early Atlantean customers to the Fleetline, there were others who were building up significant Atlantean fleets. Some municipalities took early Atlanteans and stayed with them: Hull, Newcastle, Plymouth, Portsmouth and Wallasey fall into this category. Others took early Atlantean models, briefly returned to front-engined double-deckers, and came back to rear engines — but not always in Atlanteans.

The BET group companies were equally fickle. Some, as we have seen, switched to the Fleetline to get true lowheight buses; others went in for a bit of multi-sourcing; others — though very few, it must be said — stayed true to Leyland. The Scottish Bus Group, for long a faithful Leyland customer, went for the Fleetline because of its low-bridge and, indeed, low-depot problems.

London Transport doubtless felt it had to sample the new rear-engined double-deckers, even while its own front-engined Routemaster was still being built in substantial quantities. LT bought 50 Atlanteans and eight Fleetlines in 1965, preferred the Daimler model and went on to build up a notoriously troublesome fleet of Fleetlines.

The problem of Daimler competition was partly solved in 1968 when Daimler (and Guy), as part of British Motor Holdings, passed into the new British Leyland monster which already had AEC and Bristol under its control. The Fleetline was allowed to continue in competition with the Atlantean and the Bristol VRT. Although there had been a swing towards rear-engined single-deckers in the 1960s, one-man double-deckers were legalised in 1966 and this,

with the introduction of the Bus Grant scheme for approved types, plus the formation of the first four PTEs, created a new demand for double-deckers.

Leyland now controlled the double-deck market, and had eliminated the last front-engined models, but there were mumblings among some operators who were unhappy about Leyland's monopoly and who were encouraging other manufacturers to challenge this. Leyland had also eliminated single-deck competition in favour of its new National city bus, and attempts to do the same with the double-deck Titan model in 1975 came unstuck as operators stayed with tried and tested designs.

Right:
Atlantean exports covered such unlikely places as the USA, where a batch of AN68/2Ls was operated by the New York Metropolitan Transportation Authority in the late 1970s. The Park Royal body was based on the Mancunian design developed for Manchester City Transport, but featured London-style windscreens.

Below:
Glasgow Corporation and the operators which succeeded it operated Atlanteans for 40 years. In 1984 the Strathclyde PTE was in the throes of a livery change from green and yellow to orange and black.

The Atlantean had been reborn in 1972. The last PDR range models were PDR1A/1 Specials built in 1971, which represented a compromise between the PDR1A/1 model (introduced in 1967 and featuring a rationalised Pneumocyclic gearbox) and the AN68 range, introduced in 1972. Over 5,500 PDR Atlanteans had been built for the home market, and the model had been exported to Australia, India, Ireland, Portugal, South Africa and Sweden.

The AN68 came just in time. Sales were suffering and the chassis needed a boost. The AN68 featured the 153bhp Leyland O.680 engine as standard, and problems with engine cooling on the PDR series had been addressed.

The new PTEs based on the conurbations around Birmingham, Liverpool, Manchester and Newcastle were needing new buses to replace the assortment of types inherited from the municipal fleets they had absorbed. West Midlands, not surprisingly, went for the locally-built Fleetline, but the other three went for the AN68 Atlantean as their main double-deck chassis, though each bought Fleetlines as well as other non-Leyland types. Further PTEs created in 1973/4 — Greater Glasgow, South Yorkshire and West Yorkshire — were also good Atlantean customers, though South Yorkshire later turned to the Dennis Dominator. The PTEs at Greater Glasgow, Greater Manchester, Merseyside and West Yorkshire went on to build up substantial Atlantean fleets. At one stage in the late 1970s these four fleets alone had over 3,500 Atlanteans in service; the biggest, Greater Manchester, had over 1,100 and Greater Glasgow and Merseyside were not far behind with over 900 each.

The Atlantean enjoyed an Indian summer in 1981 when 670 were delivered to British operators, just a few behind MCW's best-selling Metrobus. There was an AN69 Atlantean model too, a turbocharged version developed for export customers, for even at the end of its 26-year production run the Atlantean was still attracting new orders; Indonesia, Kuwait and Manila all took Atlanteans in the 1980s. The end of Atlantean production was largely a consequence of proposed European noise and emissions legislation, but the Olympian was well up and running by 1984 when the last chassis rolled out of Leyland.

Now, 16 years later, the Atlantean is becoming a rare sight, even in those fleets where once the model reigned supreme. Good late-model Atlanteans are still prized for school contracts, but a spate of last Atlantean days in centres like Glasgow, Nottingham and Edinburgh only serves to underline that even an undeniably successful model like the AN68 has a finite life. And although the Fleetline regularly outsold the Atlantean, it was the Atlantean that tended to outlast the Fleetline, and good AN68s are still sought after by operators looking for reliability and decent capacity.

Just two weeks before writing this I was involved in Edinburgh's Last Atlantean Running Day, when Lothian ran its six remaining AN68s on service 4, and enthusiasts ran a free service on the 45 using older versions. As with many British towns and cities, the Atlantean had been a part of everyday life for many years — 34 in Edinburgh's case — and at a stroke the streets suddenly seemed empty without that familiar 680 roar.

As a model, maybe the Atlantean didn't start off too well more than 40 years ago — but by Jove it more than made up for that with the AN68!

Above:
The Atlantean became the standard choice for Grampian Transport, and late vehicles such as this would find their way into other Scottish fleets in the 1990s as Grampian expanded and evolved into FirstBus. All of Grampian's Atlanteans had Alexander bodies.

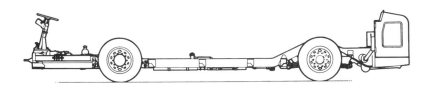

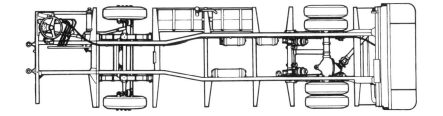

Right:
East Lancs-bodied Atlanteans were chosen by most of the Lancashire municipal fleets. Those for Preston included this coach version leaving the town's bus station, where every bus in view is an Atlantean.

Below right:
Second-hand Atlanteans introduced rear-engined double-deckers to the Isle of Man. They came from just across the water, as illustrated by a Metro-Cammell-bodied PDR1 which had been new to Liverpool Corporation.

Below:
Second-hand Atlanteans proved popular purchases in the mid-1980s as deregulation of local bus services created new opportunities for expansion. Greater Manchester disposed of large numbers of buses in 1986/7, and its Atlanteans soon turned up in fleets throughout Britain. This one didn't move far from home, and is seen in Bolton running for Ribble.

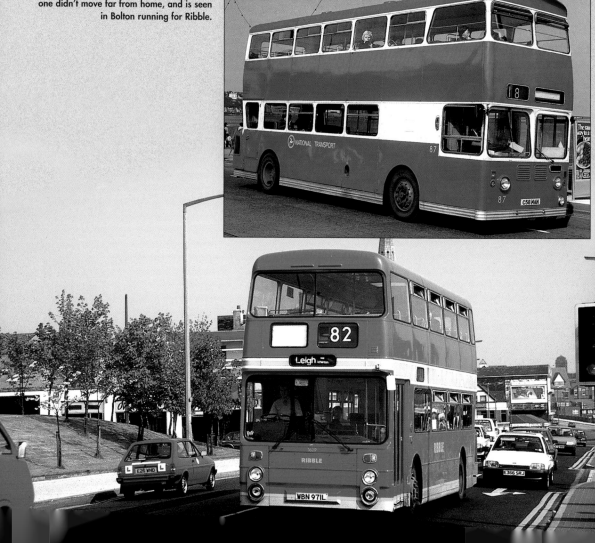

CAPITAL
CASCADE

Stephen Morris looks at the way the big groups and others are taking advantage of newish and not-so-new buses being ousted from service in London.

Left:
Titans ousted many Bristol VRs in Stagecoach South territory; this one, with South Coast Buses, is at Hastings. Terry S. Blackman

Below:
A transfer within Stagecoach; one-time London Leyland Titan T1079 is now an open-topper with Stagecoach Western Buses at Dunoon, in full Stagecoach livery. Murdoch Currie

Throughout much of the postwar period London Transport has been a fertile source of used buses for provincial operators to tap. This has been down to a number of policy reasons emanating from London over the period; for instance, a miscalculation of the number of buses which would be required meant that RTs, especially non-standard types, were sold off prematurely in the late 1950s and early 1960s. Numbers of buses to take over tram and trolleybus services, not surprisingly, failed to take into account the decline in public transport usage which set in during the first half of the 1950s, and is only now beginning to bottom out.

Traditionally, independent operators were the main users of time-expired rolling stock discarded by the larger concerns, but the sudden availability of comparatively youthful, well-maintained and well-specified urban buses meant that operators in other sectors of the industry were happy to take discarded RTs; operators such as Dundee and Bradford Corporations were amongst those happy to take advantage of LT's error of judgement.

It was something of an irony that, having discarded some RTs prematurely, LT kept the type in service until 1979, long after early postwar buses had disappeared from the rest of the country. However, it was well behind the rest of the country in moving towards one-person operation, believing the intensity and usage of its service still justified the retention of conductors. In this it was to some extent justified, and, even now, certain heavily-used central London routes are best served by crew-operated buses — even if, in 1979, there were crew-operated suburban routes which were little different from

services elsewhere which worked adequately with driver-only operation.

It has to be said that LT made something of a fist of converting to one-person operation. Perceiving a need for single-deckers for one-person operation, it bought large quantities of AEC Merlins and Swifts, just at a time when operators throughout the country were learning the shortcomings of such designs. Certain basic misunderstandings, about the structural needs of vehicles with the engine cantilevered at the end of a long rear overhang, and of the mechanical problems of packaging engines and gearboxes together in tight spaces out of the natural flow of cooling air, were beginning to bring about disastrous reliability and expensive premature structural failures on such buses elsewhere, but LT persisted in introducing them.

Having made one such blunder, it went on to introduce one-person double-deckers, based on the Daimler Fleetline. The Fleetline generally enjoyed a good reputation as a rear-engined double-decker, but LT's own specification for it, plus a reluctance to adapt maintenance procedures designed for a totally different generation of bus, meant that both types were doomed to premature withdrawal. Not many UK operators queued up to relieve LT of Swifts and Merlins — many were exported at prices which must have made a nonsense of any sensible provision for depreciating them — but the DMS-type Daimler Fleetlines were a different proposition. Many British operators found the DMS to be basically a good bus, particularly if some of LT's foibles were stripped out of them.

In the current era, buses built for London Transport use are coming out of service prematurely for very different reasons. The way London's bus services are provided was changed fundamentally by the London Regional Transport Act of 1984. LT was no longer directly responsible for providing buses; instead it was responsible for providing bus services, and private operators could compete for the privilege of actually operating them to LT's specification. Dogmatic ideas on engineering had to take second place to supplying buses which would do the job reliably and economically; the lower the costs of providing the service, the higher the profit to the operator and, for the most part, operators provided buses which were built to standard manufacturers' specifications and which were tried and tested.

At the same time, experiments were being tried throughout the country in using smaller, more cost-effective buses on higher frequencies and, while LT was to lead the way in moving up to heavier-duty, larger minibuses than those then being run in the provinces, these were still built on well-proven van bases, primarily the Mercedes 811D. While early contracts tended to go for the cheaper option of secondhand buses for routes needing large vehicles — ironically often fulfilled by LT's own unloved DMS type — later contracts often called for new buses, and contracts were awarded on the basis usually of five years.

As this process has accelerated, so has the supply of youthful and middle-aged London buses to the provincial market. By 1993 all the former London Transport operators were in the private sector, many of them in the hands of bus groups with interests already established outside the capital. The second generation of one-person

Left:
With another Stagecoach operator is a less usual cascade from London; Stagecoach Kingston-upon-Hull 927 is a Northern Counties-bodied Leyland Olympian new to Selkent for Bexleybus services, and reached its present owner via Busways. David Longbottom

Top:
MTL replaced Atlanteans with a fleet of 200 Titans; former T354 works a Lancashire Travel service in Warrington. Production difficulties with Titans in their early days meant that the major metropolitan areas were buying Atlanteans when Titans — which could have suited their needs rather better — were going into service in London. It is ironic that 15 years later they should fulfil a role in Merseyside. G. P. Senior

Above:
Go-Ahead's London companies are not in areas where Titans traditionally ran, so it has cascaded Metrobuses to the North East . Former M215 makes a not-very-new addition to the OK Travel fleet, which itself has since disappeared. David Longbottom

double-deckers in London — the Leyland Titan
and MCW Metrobus — were very much better
thought-out than the DMS had been, and the loss
of contracts to other operators — or even the
retention of contracts by the former LT operators
on the basis of supplying new buses — meant
that all of a sudden there were many surplus
Titans and, to a lesser extent Metrobuses, all with
plenty of life left in them, that could do a turn
elsewhere.

There is little doubt in the minds of most
passengers that the Titan is a more desirable bus
than the Metrobus. It was designed with much
thought for what Leyland called 'human factors',
with a low, flat floor, lots of headroom,
independent front suspension to lower the floor
and to improve ride quality, and very effective
noise suppression. So good was the suspension system
that it has formed the basis of the suspension on all of
Volvo's latest low-floor bus models.

In contrast, the Metrobus seems less competent, with a
rougher ride quality and more gloomy interior, and
sounding rather like a Gardner-engined vacuum cleaner.
It also had a tendency to fall apart around the rear end,
though not in a way which was so disastrous as to lead to

premature withdrawals. Once the rear ends had been
rebuilt it was actually a more rugged bus than the Titan,
and was built with easily-obtained parts with less
specialisation than those of the Titan. Thus withdrawals
tended to be concentrated on the Titan rather than the
Metrobus; by the start of 2000, fewer than 400 Titans
remained, as opposed to about 1,000 Metrobuses —
though those were about to diminish as low-floor double-
deckers streamed in. This in turn provided a highly

desirable second-hand bus for provincial operators to use as a replacement for more basic vehicles in their fleets.

Merseybus, privatised through the means of MTL Trust Holdings, was one operator which had not addressed the problem of replacing its fleet during the 1980s and acquired 200 Titans. After arduous service in London, they needed fairly major refurbishment, and MTL set up a production line at its massive (and by then grossly under-utilised) Edge Lane works in Liverpool, which took out the centre door and otherwise adapted the Titan to take on a new role on Merseyside. In fact, the Titans were not much newer than the ageing Atlanteans which MTL needed to replace, yet those refinements already mentioned were not features of its current fleet and, while the registration letters may have given away the fact that these 'new' buses were not so new as all that, they offered a level of refinement to the passenger and an improvement in the driver's environment which the Atlantean, good old war-horse as it might be, couldn't match.

Traditionally, the Titan was a bus to be found in north and east London, while south and west London were Metrobus territory. These distinctions were to become less absolute as time went by, but still held good in a general sense. Thus when Stagecoach acquired East London and Selkent it acquired fleets dominated by Titans. Again, Stagecoach was to find that, with influxes of new Olympians needed to fulfil LT contract obligations, it had surplus Titans which could upgrade those of its provincial fleets with pressing needs for fleet replacement. In many ways, the Titan is an ideal replacement for the

Bristol VRT, at least in locations not hampered by low bridges. It uses the same engine, a similar gearbox and, although the Titan has a complex cooling system, something very similar was used, as part of the Titan's development, on the Series 3 VRT. This was a type of which Stagecoach had inherited plenty with its acquisition of National Bus Company operators, and Titans were quickly used to replace them in Stagecoach's operations on the south coast.

Left:
Some of London Central's small batch of Leyland Olympians brought welcome upgrading to Rossendale's fleet. This is former L93 at Bacup. W. M. Ewing

Below left:
Not only Titans came up to Merseyside from London. When MTL took over London Northern, it also gained surplus Metrobuses and, a little later, more modern Alexander-bodied Scanias. Not that J-registered Scania S21, seen in Liverpool when less than five years old in 1996, looks in the peak of condition. G. S. O'Brien

Below:
Now Dennis Darts are being replaced in London, these too are migrating throughout the country. This Wright-bodied Dennis Dart — unusually with single-piece windscreen — is ex-East London RW47 and in this view has become Stagecoach Oxford 747. John Marsh

Other places needing similar replacements were United Counties, Transit in the North East, which had large quantities of ageing Fleetlines, and Western in Scotland, which had built up a fleet of secondhand Atlanteans to fulfil some of its double-deck requirements in addition to running Fleetlines. Further Titans went to Fife to strengthen its double-deck stock.

A further need for a rapid influx of double-deckers came with the acquisition of Transit Holdings' operations in Devon. The philosophy of Harry Blundred's Transit operations and those of Stagecoach were diametrically opposed; Harry Blundred's great vision of hordes of small buses was not Stagecoach's way, the latter preferring to carry the largest loads it could as a way to improve productivity. Thus, when Stagecoach reintroduced double-deckers to the

minibus land of Devon, Titans rather than more expensive new Olympians fitted the bill.

Despite Stagecoach's pride in its corporate stripes, surprisingly often Titans were pressed into service still in London red; the Devon ones in particular had tired red paint after years in London, yet with nice fresh red paint on the area where the centre door had been removed!

By contrast, Go-Ahead Group had acquired two south London operators, London General and London Central, so was blessed with a surfeit of Metrobuses rather than Titans. Go-Ahead was already a user of discarded London buses; Oxford, which has operations in many ways very similar to London's, had found the Titan a useful tool for replacing older buses and had built up a fleet of 26. Indeed, these were later to create a second wave of London cast-offs, when they too were replaced by new buses and most passed to independents. From having been a type seldom seen outside London, the Titan had become remarkably widespread! However, Metrobuses being displaced from service in London have again proved useful for replacing Bristol VRTs in the North East. Here there is already a long tradition of using highbridge buses, with few low bridges on major routes. Possibly the benefits of Metrobuses to passengers in the North East are less immediately apparent than those of Titans elsewhere; apart from air suspension, their charms are not instantly noticeable as being any greater than those of a highbridge Bristol VRT. They do, however, make life considerably easier for the driver, to whom it is clear from the outset that here is a bus of a quite different generation.

CentreWest and First Capital, meanwhile, have been sending Metrobuses off to other parts of the FirstGroup empire, again primarily as Bristol VRT replacements; notable recipients include Western National, where they appear most incongruous, and First Hampshire, which inherited a particularly elderly fleet from Southampton Citybus.

Arriva too has operations in Metrobus country, and has used this type for cascading. Here, the rationale has been less immediately obvious. Again, quite elderly Metrobuses, converted to single-door and refurbished, have replaced Atlanteans — in some cases actually newer than the Metrobuses — in Colchester. Metrobuses have also ousted much newer Leyland Olympians and Dennis Arrows from whatever it is that Arriva now calls the old London & Country; it has hardly been a positive move for passengers, especially as many of these went into service in faded red livery — still (in many cases) with yellow stripes from the Cowie era. The newer double-deckers have gone elsewhere within Arriva. A refurbishment programme has been undertaken on the Metrobuses at Arriva London North's Enfield garage to convert them to single-door and to improve the interiors, with current Arriva standard moquette seating. They have also, of course, been repainted in ubiquitous Arriva livery. Why, you may wonder, has such a move been made? It's all down to economics; marginal services in Surrey and Sussex can more easily be maintained by buses which have virtually no book value than by ones worth five or six figures. That, at least, is the accountants' logic. Others have stayed more locally, with East Herts & Essex, on services out from London's northern fringes towards Hertford. More logical has been the transfer of Metrobuses to Arriva Scotland West for school use, though Northumbria has also had some.

Arriva also has another source of ex-London double-deckers of a newer generation. London & Country bought large numbers of Volvo Citybuses with East Lancs and Northern Counties bodywork for London use (many transferring to the Londonlinks operation set up specifically to run London tendered services) which have found new uses with Arriva's urban operations in the West and East Midlands, Glasgow and the North West of England. Indeed, many were transferred well before Arriva's new identity was introduced, and appeared in Midland Red North and Bee Line liveries. Meanwhile, Arriva Scotland West received some Volvo Citybuses (still in Grey-Green livery) from Arriva London North East which it put into use on schools work, albeit with the

expectation of their being refurbished and going on to normal service.

Yet more surprising buses to find their way north are the pioneering low-floor Scania N113CRLs which began life on the 144 service (Edmonton Green-Muswell Hill Broadway) in 1993; these have been replaced by low-floor double-deckers and now serve the Trafford Centre, in Greater Manchester, and the Runcorn Busway.

London's obsession with the minibus was fairly short-lived; although there are still minibus operations, in many cases the Dennis Dart has ousted minibuses. As noted before, London redefined the minibus by moving to the larger Mercedes-Benz 811D with Alexander bodywork. One of the greatest shortcomings of this type was its poor ride quality, addressed in London by a campaign to

Above left:
Several ex-London Darts are now in Stagecoach service in Devon; some, like 786 (former East London DW71) have Wright bodywork. Philip Wallis

Left:
Out of all the FirstGroup companies, Eastern Counties has been the one needing most urgent attention in terms of fleet renewal, and middle-aged buses have been drafted in from all over FirstGroup to replace rather older ones. Some came from CentreWest, where, amongst other things, some of the very last Olympians built were at the head of a complex cascading process. This ex-CentreWest Wright-bodied Dart, DW20, is now 496 in Eastern Counties' Great Yarmouth Blue Bus fleet.
J. Podgorski

Above:
Meanwhile, half a dozen Darts with Stagecoach Devon have Carlyle bodywork. Ex-Selkent DT34, seen at Cullompton in May 1998, is one such. Mark Bailey

retrofit air suspension on the rear, to excellent effect. Most of the MA-class Alexander-bodied Mercedes went to CentreWest, firstly for the controversial replacement of Routemasters on the inner London 28 and 31 services, from which they were quickly ousted. FirstGroup's acquisition of CentreWest saw these dispersed throughout the country on FirstGroup operations; they can be found in Cornwall with Western National as well as in Greater Glasgow and central Scotland, where their registrations as applied by Alexander seem far more appropriate.

CentreWest also had a penchant for Renault S75s with Wright or Reeve Burgess bodywork. The 35 with Reeve Burgess bodywork were sold *en masse* to the Yorkshire Traction group, many of them for use on rural services in Lincolnshire — work which is not too arduous for this generally not terribly successful type of bus. They settled down well to it, but are now rather showing signs of reaching their sell-by (or sell-for-the-second-time-by) date. The 90 Wright-bodied ones have generally remained within FirstGroup, many straying only as far as neighbouring First Beeline where they provided a modern, if barely adequate, replacement for ancient Leyland Nationals. Suggestions that the Renaults were less than adequate were often countered by CentreWest, which stressed what fine buses they were — although the operator hasn't seemed too keen to keep them. Mind you, things move on quickly and First CentreWest has since cascaded sizeable quantities of Wright Handybus-bodied Dennis Darts to other FirstGroup operators, including First Beeline — and also First Eastern Counties, which has been updating its elderly fleet as quickly as possible by acquiring almost anything it can lay its hands on within FirstGroup. Other lucky recipients of Renault S75s included Leicester Citybus, which put them into service in battered ex-London condition before tidying them up and repainting them.

Further changes in London are making yet more modern types redundant. Arriva's Volvo Citybuses have already been cited, but the move to low-floor buses is also having its effect. The introduction of the Dennis Dart SLF almost overnight made the conventional Dart seem dated — and indeed early ones, now getting on for 10 years old, are reaching the end of their lives. Metroline was an early operator to make

Carlyle-bodied Darts available, and many of these were bought straight from service by one of the few remaining Lancashire municipal operators, Rossendale. The same operator seized the opportunity to relieve London Central of 10 of its 15 ECW-bodied Leyland Olympians, the last class of LT-specified double-deckers. Most of these were in service with South London (now Arriva London South) and Selkent, and the resulting small batch exiled with South London were non-standard to that operator. Again, Rossendale pressed them into service in London condition, but later converted them to single-door and refurbished them. Subsequently, while Arriva London South is hanging on to its sizeable fleet of Olympians, refurbishing them and upgrading them with Voith transmission,

Stagecoach Selkent has sent some of its Olympians to Stagecoach Midland Red (some calling in at Oxford for a while on the way) and East Kent. The rest of the batch went for sale through Ensign — once associated with selling the DMS class in the 1980s — such that none now remains with the London operator. Indeed the L-class Leyland Olympian is an endangered species, with late-model examples sold off by London United following its loss of the 140 (Heathrow-Harrow Weald) to Metroline; nine of these are with East Yorkshire, an avid collector of used Olympians.

Stagecoach, meanwhile, has also cascaded Wright-bodied Darts to ex-Transit Holdings fleets in Oxford and Devon to replace minibuses — although the traffic has

Far left:
The North East became a repository for three groups' London cast-offs, such as this ex-Kentish Bus Greenway, now with Arriva North East. A. D. Glen

Inset (left):
Arriva has cascaded former London & Country Volvo Citybuses as well as buses from the 'red' London companies. This East Lancs-bodied Citybus moved from the former Londonlinks operation to Arriva Derby.

Top:
Rather closer to its original home, but in Arriva 'provincial' livery, is Metrobus M419, running with what was County Bus and is now Arriva East Herts & Essex. Ex-London Metrobuses are being used to 'upgrade' a number of fleets in the Home Counties, despite some of them knocking on towards 20 years old. Philip Wallis

Above left:
Arriva North West has benefited from some rather newer London cast-offs, in the form of the prototype Scania N113 low-floor buses originally at Wood Green for the 144. Former SLW14 is seen with Arriva North West on the Runcorn Busway. Philip Lamb

not all been one-way; ex-Oxford two-door Darts have finished up in East London in response to a move by LT towards dual-doors even for smaller buses. Others have gone to Hastings with South Coast Buses, while an influx of 66 Plaxton-bodied Dennis Dart SLFs was due to set more London Darts rolling into other Stagecoach fleets. East Midland, for instance, was set to receive 22 to see off its Leyland Nationals, while others are bound for Fife, Western and Transit.

As low-floor double-deckers sweep into London, yet newer buses are departing for pastures new. London Central's 24 Optare Spectras, ousted from the 3 (Oxford Circus-Crystal Palace) by Connex's new Dennis Tridents, have found their way within the Go-Ahead Group to the North East, while some of Stagecoach East London's Scania double-deckers have moved down to East Kent.

For better or worse, then, London's tendering system has led to a ready source of vehicles to cascade into provincial areas. Whether provincial passengers have cause to appreciate London's munificence in sending them well-specified and younger vehicles, or have cause to resent London's dumping its old rubbish on them, depends very much on the individual circumstance. H-registered Volvo Citybuses may be welcome in Derby, and the C-registered Olympians are probably an improvement over the buses they replaced in Rossendale (they may not be new, but those L-class vehicles always were very acceptable). Passengers in Bracknell may be less enamoured at losing 22-year-old Leyland Nationals

in favour of eight-year-old Renault S75 minibuses, and i Crawley it is hard to appreciate the charms of a V-suffix Metrobus over an N-prefix Dennis Arrow. But at least it's the sort of thing that helps the world go round if you're a bus enthusiast!

Above:
Most of FirstGroup's cascaded buses from London have been smaller vehicles; this MA-class Alexander-bodied Mercedes 811 is with First Glasgow. J. S. Copeland

Below:
At almost the opposite extreme from Glasgow, another ex-CentreWest MA-class Mercedes, still in London livery, drops into Boscastle, Cornwall, in service with Western National.
DWR Picture Library

MCW was one of the big names in bus bodybuilding; then, in the 1970s, it started to concentrate on building integrals. Stewart J. Brown charts the company's final years.

THE LAST YEARS OF MCW

They were catchy names: Metrobus, Metroliner, Metrorider. They were very much products of their time — a London double-decker, a high-capacity motorway coach, and a minibus. And they were to mark the end of the road for a company which had been one of Britain's biggest bus builders — Metro-Cammell.

But let's start with the Leyland National. Like it or loathe it, the National was the bus which marked a significant change in bodybuilders' attitudes towards Britain's biggest chassis-maker. When Leyland ceased in-house bus body manufacture in 1954, it became the main source of chassis for most of the country's coachbuilders and its position grew ever stronger as what had been simply Leyland Motors evolved into the unwieldy British Leyland Motor Corporation.

The launch of the integral Leyland National and the accompanying withdrawal from sale of the Leyland organisation's rear-engined single-deck bus chassis in the early 1970s (except where it was expedient to keep them) was an important factor in Metro-Cammell's decision to co-operate with Scania in the development of the Metro-Scania. The National quickly became the standard urban single-deck bus and, despite what might be deemed an indifferent reception to the integral concept, Leyland announced that it was developing an integral double-decker. This was project B15, which was launched in 1977 as the Titan. Metro-Cammell had, meanwhile, developed a double-decker jointly with Scania — the Metropolitan. It had appeared in 1973 and won orders from a number of major fleets. Output totalled 662 when production ceased at the start of 1978.

In 1978 Strathclyde Regional Council organised a public transport event which attracted modern vehicles from local operators and was also supported by the major manufacturers. MCW provided this Metrobus, one of 12 being delivered to the China Motor Bus Co, repainted in the colours of Alexander (Midland), which would become the biggest Scottish buyer of Metrobuses, albeit with Alexander bodywork.
All photographs by the author

For Metro-Cammell in the mid-1970s the threat was clear. Walk down its production lines and every chassis being bodied came from the Leyland organisation. And Leyland was planning to replace these chassis — Atlanteans, Fleetlines and VRTs — with a new integral model. What future would that leave for Metro-Cammell? Certainly not a bright one.

The answer was to fight fire with fire.

Metro-Cammell had plenty experience of building integrated structures. Before its involvement with Scania it had worked closely with Leyland in the 1950s with the Olympic single-decker and with early Atlanteans. Before that it had built chassis-less trolleybuses for London. So it wasn't exactly a newcomer to the concept of an integral vehicle.

And so was born the Metrobus. It was developed — as was Leyland's competing Titan — with London Transport's needs very much in mind. Thus from the start the Metrobus was available with hydraulic brakes for LT, although air brakes were an option and were specified by most buyers outside London. Metro-Cammell had bodied just over 1,000 of LT's DMS family of Fleetlines, and the new Metrobus body was not unlike that fitted to the Fleetline in overall appearance. It had asymmetric windscreens, a feature carried over from the Metro-

Scania and Metropolitan, although with less of a difference in the depth of the two screens than on the earlier models. The logic was that the deeper nearside screen gave the driver a better view of the pavement. To suit LT the Metrobus was, of course, available with two doors — a layout still favoured by London in the late 1970s although it had been given up by most other urban operators.

At the launch MCW advertised a range of engine and gearbox options. The 177bhp Gardner 6LXB was to prove the most popular, but there was a 180bhp Rolls-Royce Eagle option which found a few takers. The new Cummins L10 was made available from 1983. The standard gearbox was the Voith, which had an integral retarder, but a GKN-SRM unit was offered too, although none were sold. Air suspension was fitted.

The standard bus was 9.6m long on a 4950mm wheelbase and it was this which would account for the vast majority of sales. This was known as the 95MDR, although the designation wasn't widely used. The 111MDR was 11.2m long and had a 6550mm wheelbase. An intermediate 10.45m model was later added.

LT, which would be the biggest buyer of the Metrobus, placed an initial order for five, the first of which entered service in 1978. This was soon followed by an order for

200 in 1978/9, and a further 200 in 1979/80. Leyland's problems in building Titans led to a windfall for MCW which got an order from LT for an extra 100 in 1980. The LT Metrobuses were of two-door layout and seated either 67 (on early buses with automatic fare-collection equipment) or 71 (on most later vehicles).

Other big fleets showed early interest in the new MCW model. Greater Manchester ordered 10 in 1977, a figure soon increased to 80. It was the autumn of 1979 before any arrived but, as in London, Leyland's inability to build Titans led to increased business for MCW in Manchester, which in 1979 doubled its Metrobus order to 160.

The West Midlands PTE placed an initial order for five and in February 1978 was the first operator to put one of its own Metrobuses into revenue-earning service. The first was allocated to Washwood Heath garage, which was barely a spanner's throw from MCW's factory should any problems arise. The fifth of West Midlands' Metrobuses was exhibited at the 1978 Commercial Motor Show, and a further 75 were ordered, soon increased to 175 and then to 275 when Leyland's problems with the Titan (135 of which had been on order for West Midlands) became apparent. West Midlands tried two Rolls-Royce-powered Metrobuses, but standardised on the Gardner 6LXB although it did take 20 more Rolls-Royce versions in 1981 when Gardner engines were in short supply.

Far left:
In the early days of Metrobus production, a number of fleets bought small batches or, as in the case of Tayside, a single bus for evaluation. The Tayside bus, new in 1979, had a short life in Dundee, being sold in 1985 in the interests of fleet standardisation.

Inset (top):
With the Metrobus, MCW found a new customer in Greater Manchester, which had previously bought chassis mainly from Leyland, and bodies from Park Royal and Northern Counties. A simplified livery was adopted which used more orange and less white.

Inset (below):
Alexander provided the bodywork for all of the Metrobuses delivered to the Scottish Bus Group, as shown by an Alexander (Midland) vehicle loading in Falkirk bus station.

Below:
Alexander bodywork was specified by three of the PTEs for a minority of their Metrobus intake — Strathclyde, Merseyside and, as seen here in suburban Leeds, West Yorkshire. The PTE Metrobuses had full-height versions of Alexander's R-type body; those for SBG were lower-built.

Other early users included the other five PTEs — Greater Glasgow, Merseyside, South Yorkshire, Tyne & Wear and West Yorkshire — and the National Bus Company, which took five for its Maidstone & District subsidiary in 1980. The M&D buses included examples with hydraulic brakes and two with Rolls-Royce engines. Five more followed for Bristol Omnibus later that year, along with 15 for Northern General. However, NBC still had financial links with Leyland's manufacturing operations and it was no surprise that the ECW-bodied Olympian became the group's standard.

While most of MCW's efforts were directed at selling complete Metrobuses, the company did offer the underframe to other bodybuilders. The first went to the Scottish Bus Group, which took three which were bodied by Alexander and entered service with the group's Alexander (Midland) subsidiary in Glasgow. SBG would go on to order a total of a further 136 Metrobuses, all with Alexander's new R-type body. Most were for Alexander (Midland), but among the final deliveries in 1987 were some for the newly-formed Kelvin and Strathtay companies.

The Greater Glasgow PTE, after taking an initial batch of five complete buses in 1979, added 15 with Alexander bodywork in 1982. The West Yorkshire PTE took 10 standard Metrobuses in 1980, and followed these with 10 Alexander-bodied buses in 1982. Five Alexander-bodied buses joined the Leicester City Transport fleet in 1983 and operated in the colours of Gibson of Barlestone, a business acquired in 1979. The Merseyside PTE also took 10 Alexander-bodied buses in 1982 (following five

Top:
The Mk II Metrobus was of perhaps a rather less pleasing style than the original with its peaked dome and flat-glass windscreens. The biggest buyer was West Midlands; a Mk II loads in Coventry in the summer of 1987.

Above:
A MetroBus Metrobus. The West Yorkshire PTE coined MetroBus as a fleetname, seen here on a Mk II MCW in Leeds. This bus has curved windscreens, an option specified by a small number of Mk II buyers.

Right:
In 1987 MCW tried to interest Grampian Transport in the Metrobus, and provided a West Midlands vehicle for evaluation. Grampian was to buy only one more batch of double-deckers — 10 Olympians the following year — before switching to single-deckers.

complete Metrobuses in 1979/80) as part of a comparative trial involving Dennis Dominators, Ailsas and Olympians. Merseyside had Rolls-Royce engines in five of its Metrobuses.

The only other bodybuilder to body the MCW chassis was Northern Counties, which built 30 for the Greater Manchester PTE in 1986/7. The PTE by this time had 190 complete MCW products but was anxious to maintain employment at Northern Counties — which was in PTE ownership at this time — against a background of falling orders.

A Mk II variant of the Metrobus was introduced in 1982. The mechanics remained unchanged, but the body was simplified with fewer different parts — MCW claimed the number of different components was reduced by 60%, which sounded impressive whatever it meant. The Mk II had revised glazing and a plainer style of front end with equal-sized flat glass windscreens. Most Metrobus operators — the only real exception was London — immediately switched to the Mk II. The last provincial examples of what retrospectively became the Mk I were delivered to Greater Manchester in the summer of 1983. The very last Mk Is entered London service in 1985 — and brought LT's fleet of these to 1,440. All were Gardner-powered, apart from 22 Cummins-engined buses delivered in 1984.

The Strathclyde PTE (as Greater Glasgow had become) took 25 Mk IIs in 1983, including two with Cummins engines. The last Scottish Metrobuses were 25

Mk IIs for Strathclyde in 1989 — a further 25 had been ordered but were cancelled in the light of the doubts then hanging over MCW's future. West Yorkshire took 20 Mk IIs in 1983 (plus 40 in 1984/5), while West Midlands, which had 442 Mk Is, took 689 Mk IIs between 1982 and 1989. Britain's first guided busway in Short Heath, Birmingham, was served by West Midlands using 14 Mk II Metrobuses fitted with lateral guide-wheels. Wearing 'Tracline 65' livery, they entered service in October 1984 and ran on the busway until its closure three years later.

NBC bought a number of Mk IIs. Northern General took 10 in 1983, with the engine order split equally between Gardner and Cummins. Ten went to Maidstone & District in 1984, joining the company's five earlier buses. Northern General went on to buy a further 31 Mk II Metrobuses in 1984, followed by a final 41 in 1986, including 11 with 72 coach seats (instead of 77 bus seats) which were used on Expresslink services and had Gardner 6LXDT engines. Coach-seated Mk IIs for limited-stop services were also ordered by Reading, South Yorkshire and West Midlands.

The final Metrobuses for NBC were 16 delivered to Yorkshire Traction in 1986 which were built to an overall height of 13ft 8½in compared with the standard 14ft 4in. The height reduction was achieved by cutting interior headroom and using a different, thinner structure for the upper-saloon floor. This batch of low Metrobuses remained unique.

London did eventually buy Mk IIs. Two were purchased for evaluation in 1984 with different drivetrain combinations — one Gardner/Voith, the other fitted with a Cummins L10 and the short-lived Maxwell automatic gearbox. (A third, planned to be an improved Metrobus III, was never built.) A further 27 were leased for the Harrow Buses operation in 1987, and were soon joined by two more which were diverted from an East Kent order. These operated in Harrow for three years and were returned to the leasing company when Harrow Buses lost the contracts for the services on which they were operating. They soon found new homes.

The only independent operators to buy new Metrobuses were East Kent with two batches in 1988/9, in the brief period between ownership by NBC and Stagecoach, and Ensign Bus, which received 16 two-door Mk IIs in 1988/9 for operation on London Transport contracts.

As demand for new buses started to fall in the mid-1980s, Leyland discussed with MCW the possibility of MCW abandoning the Metrobus design and instead building bodies on Leyland's Olympian chassis. MCW declined. The boot was very soon on the other foot. When the Government announced in 1986 that it planned to sell Leyland Bus, MCW's parent, the Laird Group, was among those interested in bidding — apparently with Government backing. But that, too, came to naught.

Deliveries of Metrobuses to British operators in the early 1980s were typically just over 400 a year, with a peak of almost 650 in 1981. The model's worst year was 1987, when demand for new double-deck buses took a nose-dive and just 39 Metrobuses entered service.

Inset (top left):
South Yorkshire had Mk II Metrobuses with curved screens and split-step entrances — a layout designed to make boarding and alighting easier for infirm travellers.

Inset (above left):
NBC was the biggest buyer of the impressive Metroliner double-decker, typified by a 79-seat West Yorkshire coach sweeping into central Manchester on its way to Liverpool. The vast majority of NBC Metroliners were in National Express white.

Left:
Sadly, on the motorway network the Metroliner could as often be found on the hard shoulder as in the fast lane. Two fitters can be seen under the front of this coach from the Bristol-based Wessex National company which on a run to Hull has come to grief on the M5 near Stroud.

Coaches

Britain's coach operations were deregulated in 1980, and this saw the virtual monopoly enjoyed by National Express being challenged by new operators. Part of the National Express response was to explore the benefits of running high-capacity coaches. After briefly considering and quickly rejecting articulated vehicles, National Express tried a solitary long-wheelbase Olympian coach before settling on a new three-axle double-deck design from MCW — the Metroliner.

This was an impressive-looking vehicle, with styling not unlike Van Hool's contemporary Astromega double-decker. It was powered by a transversely-mounted 290bhp Cummins L10 engine linked to a Voith four-speed gearbox and was unveiled at the 1982 Motor Show. The chassis was developed from the Super Metrobus being supplied to Hong Kong, but with a lowered driving position and improved instrumentation as befitted a high-quality coach. NBC placed an initial order for 39 Metroliners and these entered service in 1984 on services to London from a variety of places, including Bournemouth, Bristol and Manchester. More followed in 1985. The Scottish Bus Group had 12 — three at Alexander (Northern), three at Western SMT and six at Eastern Scottish — intended primarily for services to London. Three other buyers also bought Metroliners for London services. The Tyne & Wear PTE took six for its Armstrong-Galley service from the North East to the capital, while London Coaches and the West Midlands

PTE had seven between them for a joint service linking London and Birmingham in competition with National Express.

The Metroliner was 12m long, but MCW did list shorter models — 9.7m and 10.5m — although none were built. A variety of seating layouts was available, with the choice of one or two doors; the two-door arrangement helped speed loading and unloading. Many of those built for NBC were to 'Rapide' specification and incorporated a toilet.

Dealer Stuart Johnson of Harthill was appointed a Metroliner agent with the aim of securing sales to independent operators. In 1983 Stuart Johnson was listing a double-decker at £119,000 with options such as ABS for £2,670 or a video/TV installation for £4,375. The standard specification offered by Stuart Johnson had 80

seats. The option of 69 seats plus toilet cost an extra £4,750. No double-deck Metroliners were bought by independents.

The Metroliner soon earned a poor reputation for reliability, and an MCW service van became a permanent fixture at London's Victoria Coach Station. Yet it has to be recognised that some of these vehicles were being scheduled to cover high mileages. Those run by Tyne & Wear, for example, were expected to operate 200,000 miles a year. Production totalled 128.

The original 'decker was 4.23m (13ft 10in) high at a time when the widely-accepted standard for double-deck coach operation in Europe was 4m. MCW made a virtue of this in its brochures, saying: 'A notable characteristic of the Metroliner 2-deck is the generous headroom on both decks, made possible by its 4.23 metres overall height.' But, perhaps hopeful of winning business from British operators of European shuttle services, MCW developed the Metroliner 400GT, which was 4m high.

The 400GT was an attractive integral (the original model had a separate chassis) with independent front suspension and an in-line engine. This was the massive 15.5-litre Gardner 6LYT — the biggest engine ever fitted to a British coach. There were plans to offer a 14-litre Cummins engine too. Both engines were rated at 350bhp, a record output for a British-built coach at that time. The 400GT could be had with either a ZF HP600 five-speed automatic gearbox or a manual S6-150C. It had an unladen weight in the region of 15.5 tonnes.

In the event only three 400GTs were built. The original launch vehicle was sold to West Midlands for its London

Liner service, where it was soon joined by a second vehicle. The third, in National Express colours, was for Yorkshire Traction. Independent operators on the whole favoured Neoplan's racy Skyliner, and were no doubt more confident of reasonable service support from Neoplan if a coach failed on the Continent.

Above left:
A 4m-high version of the Metroliner, the 400GT, was launched in 1986. It was a good-looking coach, but only three were built. West Midlands Travel ended up with two of them. The London Liner was a joint operation with London Transport, competing with National Express between Birmingham and the capital.

Left:
The original single-deck Metroliner was functional rather than stylish and found few buyers. Two delivered to Strathclyde were unusual in incorporating wheelchair lifts in the entrance — hence the two-piece door in place of the normal single-piece plug unit. They were used on local services in Glasgow aimed at disabled travellers, as well as on private hires.

Above:
The improved Metroliner was a stylish coach indeed, though improved looks were not in themselves enough to encourage a rush of buyers and all but four were sold to public-sector companies. East Kent bought six new.

The high-profile double-decker overshadowed the rare single-deck Metroliner. This, too, was unveiled in 1982, and had unusually square styling — if 'styling' isn't overstating the case — with a peculiar stepped line to the windscreen, which echoed the asymmetric style of the Metrobus. It was rear-engined — a 250bhp Cummins L10 — with a choice of ZF S6-90 manual or Voith or SCG automatic gearboxes. It also had a separate chassis, although no other builders were tempted to body it. Five were delivered to NBC subsidiary East Kent in 1983, and four were divided equally between SBG companies Eastern Scottish and Alexander (Northern). The only other examples of the original Metroliner were two for Strathclyde, which were unusual in being fitted with wheelchair lifts at a time when access to coaches for disabled people was not seen as a major issue.

The odd styling of the single-decker was quickly addressed and what was launched as 'The new breed' appeared in two variants for 1984 — the 3.2m-high Metroliner and the Metro Hi-Liner, which was a nominal 3.4m high. While the Hi-Liner shared the styling of the lower-built model it was structurally quite different, being an integral rather than a body-on-chassis. It had a 290bhp Cummins L10 as standard, and this higher power-rating was made an option on the standard 3.2m coach. The Metroliner was priced at £69,000; the Metro Hi-Liner at £79,500.

The facelifted model was in fact a very attractive coach, but it did little better than the original. SBG took seven in 1985/6, all for Alexander (Northern), while 14 were delivered to NBC and two went to Grampian Transport. The last two were delivered to newly-independent East Kent in 1988. The only other private-sector coach sales achieved by MCW were four Hi-Liners which went to Premier Travel of Cambridge in 1985. They were sold in 1988 to East Kent, their short life at Cambridge reflecting problems with reliability. East Kent also bought the MCW demonstrator.

MCW hinted at other engine options for its single-deck, and in particular an un-named V8 unit.

Small buses

Deregulation of local bus services led to an upsurge of interest in small buses. Most of the early vehicles were based on light van and truck chassis, and it fell to MCW to design the first purpose-built minibus for service in the

changed circumstances which faced British operators from October 1986.

This new vehicle was the integral Metrorider, launched at the 1986 Motor Show. It started life as a 7m-long 25-seater with a choice of four- or six-cylinder engines from Cummins and Perkins. Three gearboxes were listed, a ZF S5-35 manual, or automatics from Allison, the AT545, and Chrysler. The Chrysler gearbox was soon deleted from the option list. Prices in 1986 started at £26,316.

The attractive Metrorider had a welded steel frame, stretched-steel side panels, and bonded glazing. Orders were placed for 80 by Greater Manchester Buses, 50 by West Midlands Travel and 50 by coach dealer Stuart Johnson. By the end of 1987 MCW was claiming to have delivered an incredible 500 Metroriders to fleets throughout Britain. Early buyers included London Buses; the municipal fleets at Blackburn, Colchester, Darlington, Grampian, Great Yarmouth, Hyndburn, Merthyr Tydfil, Newport and Reading; NBC subsidiaries East Midland, Northumbria and South Wales Transport; and Strathclyde Buses. Scottish Bus Group subsidiary Midland Scottish, already running Metrobuses, took Scotland's first Metroriders, four delivered in 1987; they were followed by 20 for Fife Scottish. Sales to small independents included a few well-known names such as Skill's of Nottingham and Harris Bus of Grays.

Above left:
The Hi-liner shared the styling of the new-look Metroliner but was higher and was also an integral, where the lower model retained a conventional chassis; both were powered by Cummins L10 engines. MCW's demonstrator, quaintly re-registered from an A-prefix to an A-suffix number, leaves Glasgow's Buchanan bus station in 1986. It was later bought by East Kent.

Left:
The Metrorider was an instant success — even if, after an initial burst of enthusiasm, operators soon became dissatisfied with MCW's baby. Greater Manchester, facing competition from United Transport's new minibus operation, ordered substantial numbers of minibuses, including 80 Metroriders. When new they carried this eye-catching 'Little Gem' livery, but on their first repaints received the standard orange and white fleet colours.

Above:
Capitalising on the metro theme, NBC's Cheltenham & Gloucester subsidiary used the fleetname 'Metro' on its 14 Metroriders. One unloads in Cheltenham.

When it launched the Metrorider, MCW promised a bigger version and this was at the 1987 Bus & Coach show in the shape of an 8.4m-long 33-seater. Two widths were offered on the long model: 2.21m — the same as the original 7m model — and 2.38m. It had a 4750mm

wheelbase compared with the standard 4150mm. London was one of the biggest users of the original Metrorider, with 70, and became the biggest user of the stretched version, taking 63. The original London Metroriders included vehicles for Westlink, Harrow Buses and Bexleybus. The first of the longer vehicles were allocated to the Roundabout fleet in Orpington.

The stretched Metrorider soon proved to have been inadequately developed, with early reports of structural failure adding to a growing chorus of criticism from unhappy Metrorider customers. Fortunately the stretched Metrorider was bought by relatively few operators. The biggest user outside London was Strathclyde with 33. Smaller numbers were bought mainly by municipal fleets such as Blackburn, Colchester, Darlington, Great Yarmouth and Reading. Yorkshire Traction and Kentish Bus also had a few, as did a handful of small operators.

Design and construction problems with the whole Metrorider range plagued what had started off with such promise, and may have played a part in the Laird Group's disenchantment with the MCW operation.

Total output of Metroriders by MCW was just over the 1,000 mark.

Above:

The stretched Metrorider enjoyed — if that is the word — a short production life. Strathclyde Buses bought 33 new examples and also acquired some second-hand. This bus in Paisley was one of five purchased from Colchester Borough Transport in 1991 when they were just three years old. The bigger Metrorider could accommodate eight more seats than the original model.

Exports

MCW sold 540 Metrobuses in Hong Kong, initially to the two major operators, China Motor Bus and Kowloon Motor Bus. CMB built up a fleet of 136, while KMB eventually had 345. Most of these were three-axle buses, including 83 CMB buses which were 12m long and 254 for KMB which were 11m long. In addition, the Kowloon-Canton Railway had 59 two-axle Mk II buses.

The three-axle version was labelled the 'Super Metrobus' and could carry up to 124 seated passengers. Alternatively, the seating could be reduced to 110, which then left space for 60 standees. For this the engines were uprated to 212bhp for the Gardner, 220bhp for the Cummins and 230bhp for the Rolls-Royce.

MCW also tried to drum up interest in the Metrobus in Eire, with a Mk II demonstrator which was later sold to Stevensons of Uttoxeter.

In 1987 MCW reached agreement with Bova under which the Dutch manufacturer would sell Metroriders in the Low Countries, and a left-hand-drive bus was in the demonstration park at the 1987 Bus & Coach show. Only a handful were sold in Europe. Three Metroriders went to Hong Kong, two to China Motor Bus and one to Kowloon Motor Bus. Fifteen were bought by Dublin Bus.

The company briefly looked at sales in the Antipodes, advertising its Metroliner double-deck coach in Australia. None were sold there — or anywhere else outside the UK.

Another unsuccessful export model with production counted in the Metrobus 'MB' series of chassis numbers was a mid-engined single-decker. Indeed the very first

Metrobus buyers

London Transport	1471
West Midlands	1131
Kowloon Motor Bus	345
Greater Manchester	220
South Yorkshire	170
China Motor Bus	136
Midland Scottish	121
Northern General	97
West Yorkshire/Yorkshire Rider	105
Greater Glasgow/Strathclyde	70
Kowloon-Canton Railway	59
Reading	51
Merseyside	40
Kingston-upon-Hull	30
East Kent	22
Newport	16
Yorkshire Traction	16
Maidstone & District	15
Kelvin Scottish	10
Leicester	9
Strathtay Scottish	8
Bristol	5
Tyne & Wear	5
Derby	1
Tayside	1
Demonstrators	2
Total	**4156**

Small bus, big buyers

The MCW Metrorider was ordered by many big fleets, but also found its way into a large number of small firms, many just buying one or two. The main big customers for the Metrorider — each buying more than a dozen buses and together accounting for around 80% of sales — were:

London Buses	133
West Midlands Travel	85
GM Buses	80
Strathclyde Buses	75
Wilts & Dorset	75
Yorkshire Traction	51
Cardiff	46
Northumbria	45
Yorkshire Rider	39
London Country (North West)	30
Blackburn	26
South Wales	25
Fife Scottish	20
Inter-Valley Link	17
Grimsby-Cleethorpes	16
Dublin Bus	15
East Midland	15
Cheltenham & Gloucester	14
City of Oxford	14

Metroliner Production

Double-deck

Original model

London Coaches	4
NBC (102)	
Ambassador Travel	4
City of Oxford	8
Crosville	5
Devon General	3
East Yorkshire	2
Midland Fox	5
Midland Red Coaches	7
Midland Red (Express)	3
Midland Red (North)	1
National Travel (West)	10
North Devon	4
Shamrock & Rambler	14
Southern National	2
United Auto	6
Wessex	11
West Yorkshire	7
Western National	10
SBG (12)	
Eastern Scottish	6
Northern Scottish	3
Western Scottish	3
Tyne & Wear	6
West Midlands	3
400GT	
Demonstrator	1
West Midlands	1
Yorkshire Traction	1
Total double-deck	**130**

Single-deck

Original model

East Kent	5
Eastern Scottish	2
Northern Scottish	2
Strathclyde	2
Revised model	
East Kent	6
Eastern National	4
Hi-Liner	
Demonstrator	1
East Kent	2
East Midland	2
Grampian	2
Northern Scottish	7
Premier Travel	4
Wessex	2
West Midlands	1
Total single-deck	**42**

'MB' number, MB5001, was such a vehicle, which went to South Africa in 1978. A second chassis was built for a Greek operator. Coded SM — **S**ingle-deck **M**id-engine — it featured a horizontal Rolls-Royce Eagle power unit.

Decline

In the summer of 1988 MCW was developing a new model to fill a gap in its range. This was a full-size integral single-decker, and the plan was to launch it at the 1988 Motor Show. The project was put to one side — in part, perhaps, because of big Metrobus orders from KMB and West Midlands Travel for 90 and 150 vehicles respectively.

But the fate of the planned new single-decker — and of the company — was to be sealed at the end of the year when the Laird Group announced that it wanted to sell MCW — not just its bus manufacturing, but its taxi and rail businesses too. Against a background of uncertainty in the UK bus market — although the signs were that orders were picking up — no buyers were forthcoming for the business as a going concern. Early indications of problems with the Metrorider may also have played a part, with massive warranty bills and legal action on the horizon, while disillusionment over failure to acquire Leyland could have influenced Laird's decision.

Instead, the rights to manufacture specific products were sold, and the MCW bus production lines in Washwood Heath closed down. The last major deliveries of the Metrobus II in 1989 were the balance of 150 for West Midlands, 25 for Yorkshire Rider and 25 for Strathclyde Buses. Strathclyde cancelled an order for a further 25, buying Alexander-bodied Volvo Citybuses in their place. The very last vehicle by chassis number, MB10417, was the last Strathclyde Metrobus II.

Optare bought the rights to the Metrorider and the Metroliner. The former was quickly relaunched at Coach & Bus '89 as the MetroRider (with a capital 'R') and was a much-improved product which addressed items causing mounting concern among the growing band of dissatisfied MCW Metrorider users. The Metroliner quietly died, and no-one noticed.

Plaxton expressed an interest in the Metrobus design, but had just taken over the remnants of the Duple business and had also acquired the Henlys Group, and so lost interest. In the end, the rights to the Metrobus were acquired by DAF and Optare — which ultimately led to the development of the DAF DB250 double-deck chassis and the Optare Spectra body.

The demise of MCW is, of course, just part of a massive change in bus manufacturing in Britain. Other big names have gone too — Duple, ECW and Leyland, for example. Yet there's a positive side to the story too, and the manufacturers which remain are stronger than before. Henlys, owner of Plaxton, ranks among the biggest bus builders in the Western hemisphere, thanks to its ownership of North American builders Blue Bird and its interest (with Volvo) in Prevost and NovaBus. Mayflower has brought together under common ownership Dennis and Alexander, and is opening up new export markets. Wright goes from strength to strength, while East Lancs and Optare have built up a loyal following from operators outside the big groups.

The contraction of the 1980s had turned into expansion by the end of the 1990s. And there's every sign that it will continue.

MCW sold a healthy number of double-deckers to Hong Kong, including three-axle Super Metrobuses such as this example running for KMB. Based on the Mk II body, the use of deep glass for the upper-deck front windows improves the slightly unfinished look of the standard UK body. This is a 1986 102-seater.

PACKING 'EM IN!

There we all were, happily accepting that the usual seating capacity for normal double-deck buses was 56, as it had been for about 20 years, although there were some notable exceptions. It should be understood that 'normal' double-deckers in this context means highbridge, rear-entrance, two-axle, forward-engined specimens of up to 27ft length. Then everyone realised that the mid-1950s must have arrived because many buses began to enter service with considerably more than 56 seats. The passengers were certainly being packed in! There was no overnight change, of course, and broadly speaking the trend toward the highest possible seating capacity followed closely upon the start of the fashion for lightweight buses during the early-middle period of the decade. A number of operators did increase seating capacities of buses that had been in service for several years, but such alterations are disregarded in these paragraphs.

It should be understood that where the seating capacity was 56, the normal layout of the seats was:

Maximising seating capacity within legislative constraints has long been a challenge to bus operators and manufacturers. David Wayman investigates alternatives to the standard 56-seat layout for double-deckers of the 1940s and 1950s.

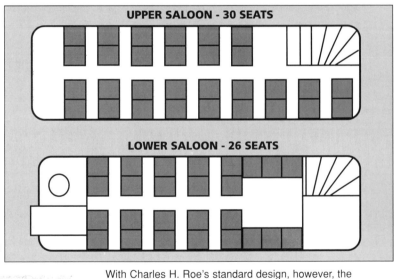

UPPER SALOON
NEARSIDE:	OFFSIDE:
9 double transverse (=18)	6 double transverse (=12)
Total: 30	

LOWER SALOON
NEARSIDE:	OFFSIDE:
5 double transverse (=10)	5 double transverse (=10)
1 triple longitudinal* (=3)	1 triple longitudinal* (=3)
*over wheel arches	
Total: 26	

With Charles H. Roe's standard design, however, the split was 31/25 due to the effect of that concern's patent 'safety' staircase with two landings, introduced in 1937 and used in peacetime-production bodies. This layout featured two steps from the platform to the first landing, then five straight steps to the second landing, then one final step up to the gangway. The staircase encroached a little into the lower saloon on the offside, robbing it of a seat which was relocated at the nearside rear upstairs in order to keep the same total as before.

Among the exceptions with less than 56 seats during the early postwar period were the 'deckers of some operators, particularly in southern England, where the reduction was artificial in that it was chosen rather than imposed by physical factors. With Southdown, for instance, the total was usually 54 (split 28/26, ie 28 in the upper saloon and 26 in the lower), the company having some East Lancs, Leyland, Northern Counties (NCME), Park Royal and Saunders bodies of this layout. At Portsmouth, the Corporation specified 52 seats for some bodies built by Crossley (28/24) and by local builder Reading (some 26/26, others 28/24). Running in Eastbourne were some examples of buses with 52-seat bodies ordered from East Lancs and its associate, Bruce (28/24), and some East Lancs and Weymann bodies seating only 50 (26/24).

Among undertakings elsewhere, Birmingham accepted a seating capacity of 54 (30/24) on Brush, Crossley, Metro-Cammell (MCCW) and Park Royal bodies as the penalty for a type of staircase that was virtually straight but of course encroached on seating space. Edinburgh and Newcastle Corporations accepted the Birmingham specification for quicker delivery of some Metro-Cammell bodies, although the Tyneside city had the layout altered to 55 seats (31/24) while the Scottish capital squeezed in 56 (31/25), which showed that it could be done. Salford Corporation asked for the Birmingham-style staircase on some Metro-Cammell and Burlingham bodies, which kept their seating capacity down to 54 (30/24), although some other Metro-Cammell bodies in the same fleet had 54 or as few as 50 seats with a normal staircase. Then there were those undertakings that had 'deckers with more than 56 seats before the mid-1950s. Some of London's early STL-class AECs were 60-seaters (34/26), and they dated as far back as 1933. Later, some provincial operators

specified seating capacities of more than 56, notably Coventry Corporation from the late prewar years and several others during the late 1940s and early 1950s, Manchester and Hull Corporations being among the earliest.

Designs with more than 56 seats were constricted by the legal gross (ie laden) weight limit or maximum length applicable at the time. Before World War 2, the restriction was chiefly the laden weight limit which for two-axle double-deck motorbuses had been increased from 10 tons to 10½ (which was typically expressed as 10 tons 10cwt 0qrs) in 1935, going up to 11 tons in 1941, then to 12 in 1946 and to 14 in 1956. Officially, the unladen weight of a bus for taxation and other purposes was the

weight of the complete vehicle excluding fuel, water, oil, loose tools and equipment. The laden weight was calculated by adding in the weight of fuel, water and oil, plus 140lb per seat (a nominal average allowance for a full seated load of passengers), plus 140lb each for the driver and conductor (140lb = 10st = 1¼cwt). This meant that 60 passengers plus two-person crew, for example, theoretically weighed 3.17.2.

In 1933/4, some double-deckers were tending to weigh nearly 6.10.0 unladen, but the 60-seat London STLs weighed less than 6.0.0 and therefore had no difficulty in keeping within the 10-ton gross limit. By 1939, however, when Coventry was specifying 60 seats, most unladen weights had crept over the 6.15.0 mark and so bodywork had to be lightened in order not to exceed the 10½-ton restriction. In early postwar years the first rise in the gross weight limit had eased the problems of increased seating capacities and the major limiting factor became length. This was still restricted to 26ft although operators would have preferred it to be greater.

Coventry's first 60-seat buses were based on a version of the 7.0-litre Gardner-engined Daimler COG5 chassis which allowed the lower saloon front bulkhead of the Brush body to be located further forward than normal and this, along with a slight repositioning backward of the rear bulkhead, increased the length of the lower saloon

sufficiently to achieve the astonishing total of 31 seats — a figure exceeded only by one seat in many 30ft-long front-engined models from 1956. The normal downstairs layout was five transverse (forward-facing) double seats per side plus one longitudinal (inward-facing) bench for three on each wheel arch, but Coventry's specification crammed in a rearward-facing bench for five with its back to the front bulkhead, then five transverse doubles per

Left:
Coventry Corporation was an eminent pioneer in higher seating capacities, starting the process prewar. This 1940 60-seat Brush-bodied Daimler COG5/60 represents the city's high-capacity, lightweight buses of the era. R. Marshall

Below left:
This deliciously raucous Hull Corporation 1946 7.7-litre AEC Regent II, representing a batch of 16, had 60 seats in its Weymann body, two more than other early postwar specimens in the same fleet. R. Marshall

Below:
Typical basic, standard, no-frills early postwar bus with popular 30/26 seating configuration: a 1946 Leyland Titan PD1 with Alexander body of Leyland design, No 4 in the Darwen Corporation fleet. H. W. Peers

side, as well as an inward-facing triple bench on each wheel arch. Paradoxically, the Coventry upper-saloon figure was artificially reduced by one to 29 in order not to exceed the total of 60 and, aside from some primitive open-staircase, short-upper-deck types, these buses may have been the only double-deckers in which the lower saloon capacity was greater than the upper. Some subsequent Metro-Cammell-bodied 7.7-litre AEC-engined Daimler COA6s placed in service by Coventry seated 31/29, which was achieved without so much structural modification. In this case, the lower-saloon seating layout differed from that of the Brush design in that the wheel-arch seats were doubles and not triples.

During the early postwar years the idea of the rearward-facing bench for five against the front bulkhead was perpetuated by Kingston-upon-Hull in some 60-seat (31/29) Weymann bodies, as well as by Edinburgh in those 56-seat (31/25) Birmingham-pattern Metro-Cammells. Then, perhaps most famously of all, it was featured in the ECW-bodied Bristol Lodekka introduced in 1949, although in that case it was not included primarily in order to maximise seating capacity.

Manchester's method of increasing the total from 56 to 58 was achieved more simply and did not incorporate any rearward-facing seats or structural alterations. All that was done was to insert an additional double seat upstairs on the offside where, in order to take up the available floor-space fairly evenly, the seats usually had a greater pitch (that is, space between back squabs in line) than the nearside ones. London's buses, however, usually did not conform to this practice as the policy there was to keep the seat pitch equal on both sides in order to position the rearmost offside seat further forward, creating greater circulation space around the staircase top. In the case of provincial buses — for example in the early postwar standard Crossley body with reasonably typical seating configuration — the seat pitch was normally 2ft 8in on the offside and 2ft 1in on the nearside. The Manchester idea was to make the offside seat pitch almost the same as the nearside one in order to create enough space for the additional double seat on the offside.

A total of 60 was also sometimes achieved by an alternative method to that used by such as Coventry and Hull. By reducing the wheel-arch seats from triples to doubles, a further transverse double could be inserted on either side ahead of the wheel arches, bringing the lower saloon total to 28, comprising 24 transverse (six doubles per side) and four longitudinal (two over each wheel-arch). With 32 upstairs, arranged Manchester-style, 60 passengers could then be seated without appreciable loss of comfort. Indeed, during postwar years, for its lowbridge requirements the Tilling (later British Transport Commission) group of companies standardised on Eastern Coach Works bodies with this seating configuration in the

lower saloon. After the maximum length of double-deckers was increased to 27ft in 1950, permitting a lengthened lower saloon, a downstairs total of 28 was achieved more conveniently by using wheel-arch seats accommodating four each, with five double transverse seats per side.

Among the earliest vehicles with this last-mentioned arrangement were some Bristol KSW-type chassis with ECW highbridge bodywork containing 60 seats (32/28). The upper saloon total of 32 in this design included a rearmost nearside seat for three with a single seat immediately in front of it, a configuration which also improved circulation space around the staircase top. Customers for this variety included BTC companies Brighton Hove & District; Bristol Tramways; Crosville; Eastern Counties; Hants & Dorset; Lincolnshire; Notts & Derby, and United.

In the other sectors, those operators acquiring new buses containing more than 56 seats between 1946 and the mid-1950s included:

OPERATOR	BODYBUILDER	SEATING TOTAL	LAYOUT
Municipalities			
Accrington	East Lancs	58	32/26
Birkenhead	Leyland, Massey	57	31/26
	East Lancs	59	31/28
Bradford	East Lancs	59	33/26
Burnley, Colne & Nelson	Leyland	57	32/25
	East Lancs	57	31/26
Coventry	Metro-Cammell	60	31/29
		58	31/27
Edinburgh	Leyland	58	30/28
Kingston-upon-Hull	Weymann	60	31/29
		58	32/26
Leeds	Roe	58	33/25
	Weymann	58	32/26
Manchester	Brush, Crossley, Leyland, Metro-Cammell	58	32/26
	Leyland, Metro-Cammell, Northern Counties	60	32/28
	Northern Counties	61	33/28
Rawtenstall	Leyland	59	31/28
Rochdale	East Lancs, Weymann	59	33/26
Sheffield	Roe	58	33/25
Southport	Weymann	58	32/26
Sunderland	Roe	58	33/25
BET COMPANIES			
East Kent	Park Royal	58	32/26
Maidstone & District	Leyland	58	30/28
	Weymann	58	32/26
Southdown	Leyland	58	32/26
Trent	Leyland	58	32/26
INDEPENDENT			
Lancashire United	Northern Counties, Weymann	57	31/26

Left:
Portsmouth Corporation was one of a minority of operators specifying fewer than 56 seats during the early postwar period, this 1949 all-Crossley DD42/7T being one of 25 that typcially were 52-seaters. Their 8.6-litre Crossley engines and torque-convertor transmissions were subsequently replaced by prewar 8.6-litre engines and conventional gearboxes of Leyland manufacture.
R. Marshall

Left:
East Kent placed in service some 58-seat Guy Arabs during the period in question, most having handsome Park Royal bodywork of an outline derived from that of the London RT family, although in this case 8ft wide. Other BET companies tended not to favour tin fronts for double deckers. David Wayman

Below:
Coventry continued with higher capacities in the immediate postwar years and this 1952 Daimler CVD6 (with Daimler 8.6-litre engine), one of 40, had a substantially-built Metro-Cammell body with Coventry's then standard seating capacity of 58. R. Marshall

The 1954 Commercial Motor Show was the principal event that drew attention to the arrival of near-maximum seating capacities. Appearing either in the exhibition hall or on the demonstration park were several 'deckers combining lightness of weight with seating capacities of more than 60. There were three 61-seaters (33/28), comprising a Park Royal-bodied AEC Regent V for Walsall Corporation and similarly-bodied AEC Regent V and Guy Arab IV demonstrators; two 64-seaters, made up of a London Transport AEC-Park Royal Routemaster (36/28) and a Metro-Cammell 'Orion'-bodied Leyland Titan PD2/20 for Edinburgh Corporation (35/29); and two 65-seat Daimler CVG5s (both 37/28), one with Northern Counties body for Walsall and the other with Roe body on Park Royal metal frames incorporating a revised design of the 'safety' staircase, creating 10in more floor space on the offside of the upper saloon, for Sunderland Corporation.

Having unladen weights of about seven tons or less, some of these vehicles were to return about 10.5mpg on urban service and so, in theory at least, were considerably more efficient tools for their job than, say, earlier eight-ton 56-seaters doing about 9.5mpg. Edinburgh's example incorporated a rearward-facing bench for five in the lower saloon, giving the total of 29. Any lower-saloon amount up to this number could be combined with any upper-saloon capacity up to the maximum of 37, as in the Walsall and Sunderland examples, to reach any total up to 66 which was the highest achievable in a double-decker of 27ft length. Or was it? Had it been feasible to achieve Coventry's prewar Brush lower-saloon capacity of 31, the total could have

been 68. Indeed, some early-1960s 27ft Massey bodies in the Birkenhead municipal fleet were to have 30 seats in the lower saloon, although the upper-saloon capacity was limited to 35 rather than 37, and clearly a rearward-facing five-seat front bench could have increased capacity downstairs to 31, thus equalling Coventry's prewar lower-saloon total.

From 1954, 'deckers containing up to 66 seats within an overall length of 27ft entered service with a wide range of operators throughout Britain. Examples with the maximum could be seen as far apart as Southampton and Aberdeen, and generally those operators serving the more densely-populated, heavily-industrialised areas were among those keenest for seating capacities of about 63 to 66.

But was there much sacrifice of comfort in the higher-capacity double-deckers? There may not necessarily have been. The table below compares the seating total and various dimensions of several fairly typical makes and designs of bodywork. (Figures quoted here may have varied between batches of bodies of each make for various customers.)

From this it will be seen that the addition of seats did not always mean significant loss of legroom. A more upright front or other means of maximising floor space for seating could affect the situation considerably. In the case of the Leyland, East Lancs, Northern Counties and Weymann bodies, the upper-saloon rearmost nearside seat was positioned some 2ft or so from the extreme rear, which of course affected the space available. Indeed, in the Weymann case, it was sufficiently far forward for only eight rather than nine rows of seats to be positioned on

BODY YEAR, MAKE AND TYPE	1951	1952	1948	1951	1957	1958	1955	1957
	Leyland	Weymann	Crossley	E Lancs	Roe	NCME	MCCW*	Burlingham
	56-seat	56-seat	58-seat	59-seat	60-seat	61-seat	64-seat	65-seat
	(30/26)	(30/26)	(32/26)	(33/26)	(33/27)	(33/28)	(36/28)	(37/28)
OVERALL LENGTH	26ft 0in	27ft 0in	25ft 5½in	27ft 0in	27ft 0in	27ft 0in	27ft 0in	27ft 0in
Upper-saloon floor								
nearside, front to rear	22ft 0½in	22ft 1in	22ft 11in	22ft 10in	23ft 10in	21ft 9in	23ft 8in	23ft 0in
offside, front to stair top	20ft 3½in	20ft 11in	20ft 0in	20ft 5in	18ft 0in	20ft 6½in	21ft 3in	21ft 2in
offside, rear seat to stair top	2ft 11in	2ft 8in	2ft 4in	2ft 9in	(a)	2ft 4in	2ft 3in	2ft 4in
Upper-saloon seats								
nearside	9x2	8x2	9x2	8x2, 1x3	8x2, 1x3	8x2, 1x3	10x2	9x2, 1x3
offside	6x2	7x2	7x2	7x2	7x2	7x2	8x2	8x2
Lower-saloon floor								
length (within bulkheads)	16ft 10in	17ft 3in	16ft 5in	17ft 3in	17ft 4in(b)	17ft 3in	17ft 3in	17ft 3in
Lower-saloon seats								
nearside	5x2, 1x3	5x2, 1x3	5x2, 1x3	5x2, 1x3	5x2, 1x4	5x2, 1x4	5x2, 1x4	5x2, 1x4
offside	5x2, 1x3	5x2, 1x3	5x2, 1x3	5x2, 1x3	5x2, 1x3	5x2, 1x4	5x2, 1x4	5x2, 1x4
Transverse seat pitch								
lower saloon	2ft 3in	2ft 3in	2ft 2in	2ft 2½in	2ft 2in	2ft 3in	2ft 2½in	2ft 3in
upper saloon nearside	2ft 1in	2ft 4in	2ft 2½in	2ft 2in	2ft 2½in	2ft 2in	2ft ½in	2ft 3in
upper saloon offside	2ft 7in	2ft 3in	2ft 2¼in	2ft 0in	2ft 1in	2ft 5in	2ft 1½in	2ft 3in

* Orion design

Notes:
a 'Safety' staircase; rearmost offside seat positioned against upper landing, ie top stair.
b Intrusion of 'safety' staircase into offside of lower saloon: 1ft 1in

Above:

The crisp, practical lines of the 60-seat body on Brighton Hove & District 6447 are typical features of the final design of Eastern Coach Works body for the Bristol K series of chassis designs, in this case a KSW6G. Its appearance may be compared with that of the more bland-looking Weymann Aurora design seen alongside.
David Wayman

Above:
The Roe safety staircase of original layout encroached 13in into the offside corner of the lower saloon, thus reducing the capacity of the offside wheel-arch seat by one as shown here. Traditionally this seat had been a double, but in this case the repositioning of the transverse seats has allowed it to be a triple, and the nearside one a quadruple, bringing the lower saloon total to 27. David Wayman

the nearside, an additional double seat being fitted on the offside to make up the deficit. With the other makes, it was about as far back as it could be but the Burlingham design, which incorporated a somewhat upright frontal profile, came out all-round best in combining maximum seating with minimum loss of comfort. Other than for passengers of much above average height, any reduction in comfort was probably more attributable to a spartan design of seat, sometimes specified in order to further reduce unladen weight. Although the introduction of 30ft-

long front-engined double-deckers in 1956, followed by rear-engined examples two years later, meant that seating capacities could rise to 78, a significant number of operators continued to order 27ft-long models until the effects of the Transport Act, 1968, rendered them obsolete.

Thanks are due to the Greater Manchester Museum of Transport for allowing access to some of the vehicles illustrated.

Left:
The operator's standard capacity during 1957-65, 66 seats were squeezed into the Metro-Cammell Orion body of this 7.7-litre AEC Regent V of Aberdeen Corporation, new in 1958. R. Marshall

Below:
Fresh from the 1954 Commercial Motor Show in London and with appropriate lettering on the window above the wheel arch, Sunderland Corporation 202, a Daimler CVG5 with Roe 65-seat (37/28) bodywork built on Park Royal metal frames, provides an example of the usual maximum seating capacity achievable without resorting to a rearward-facing bench for five passengers at the front of the lower saloon. Signwriter Bob Hedley poses for the photographer. In Roe bodies, an upper-saloon total of more than 33 could be achieved only by modifying the staircase design. Sunderland Echo

TRAVELS
THROUGH
ASIA

Michael H. C. Baker savours the
delights of the Far East.

and dust — we slept in it, we played cards in it, got to make friendships in it, fell out in it, cursed it when it broke down, blessed it as a friendly reminder of home when things got a bit too foreign, and washed it several times in rivers and water-holes which had certainly never seen a Maudslay before.

The journey would be impossible to repeat today. Not only has poor Kabul been devastated by years of bombardment and civil unrest, but we stopped off in Jerusalem, in the section of the city which then belonged to Jordan, then came down to the Mediterranean at Beirut and watched fishermen hauling in their nets at dusk, a scene straight from the Bible and which could hardly have changed in 2,000 years; next day we moved back into the 20th century by going to see *The Sound of Music*, headed eastwards over the mountains to Damascus and followed a French-built tram inching its way through the teeming crowds in the Street Called Straight, and travelled the breadth of Iraq, a country long since out of bounds to western tourists.

Even then, Iraq was an unsettling place: a public execution of Jews had been held in the main square a week before our arrival; we watched a body float down the Tigris and were told by the local police chief that his policy was to ignore it as within a couple of kilometres it would be out of his jurisdiction; and Rachel, all 5ft of her, consistently beat me at table-tennis in the Baghdad YMCA. One compensation was the rather surprising presence of red-painted Park Royal-bodied AEC Regent Vs. If one half closed one's eyes, ignored the fact that the cab was on the wrong side, forgot about the smell and the temperature, then one might — just might — have imagined oneself in Southampton.

The first bus I ever travelled upon in Asia was a Yeates-bodied Maudslay — but wait, it gets more exotic. This took me all the way from Gillingham, Kent, to Kabul, Afghanistan — well, very nearly. The Maudslay belonged to a fleet of two, the other being a Plaxton-bodied Commer. The company was the Overlanders, ie Roger, a textile engineer from Mansfield, and Janet, a nurse from Chatham.

Both vehicles contracted various tropical diseases en route but the Maudslay, which had an AEC engine, stoically survived and eventually made it to Kabul. The rather more fragile and sophisticated two-stroke Commer didn't and expired in the Iranian desert southwest of Isfahan.

My overland journey to Kabul occupied some eight weeks towards the end of 1966.

The old Maudslay became very much our home. Washing hung from seat backs, vents and other inconvenient places — at least it dried quickly in the heat,

Left:
**The Overlanders Maudslay Marathon
passes two local buses in Kabul in November 1966.**

73

It proved extremely difficult to leave the country, on account of differences between Iraq and Iran over the Kurdish problem, and eventually we had to take our Maudslay right down to the Persian Gulf and cross there. Iran was like a breath of fresh air compared to Iraq. This was in the days of the Shah; unveiled young women were an everyday sight in the capital, holding jobs of responsibility, and riding the city's taxis and buses unaccompanied. At that time Iran was a good customer of the British motor industry, and Leylands, Hillmans and Commers were imported in great numbers, some being built under licence there.

With the demise of our Commer we had to find room for all 52 of us in the Maudslay. This was an impossibility so a number of us took to local transport from Tehran onwards. Mercedes, as in so many other countries, was beginning to oust British products and it was in a virtually new Mercedes coach that I made the 350-mile journey from Tehran to the holy city of Meshed in the east of the country. The road was not tarred but our driver overcame this by pressing his accelerator hard down to the floorboards so that we flew from ridge to ridge with such speed that we avoided hitting the hollows in between — well, most of them — and our progress was thus less erratic than it might have been.

Beyond Meshed lay the Afghan border and roads which were not merely unmade but disappeared entirely in the rainy season, and out of it consisted of fairly indeterminate tracks along dried-up river-beds. The only means of public transport was huge, high-wheel trucks, mostly American

Macks. I say mostly, but that might not mean more than two or three in a day. We managed to find one heading for Herat, in Afghanistan, and off we went, the driver making great use of his vast range of gears as he eased up and down the steep river banks, around dunes and along stone-strewn tracks, occasionally taking his hands off the steering wheel to throw them in the air and declare dramatically, 'Afghanistan!'

At Herat, where local transport was provided by faded but elegant horse-drawn tongas, a beautifully-made metalled road looped across the desert for 400 miles, with the snow-covered mountains of the Hindu Kush, which merge into the Himalayas, away to the north. Now there were buses, of a sort. Essentially they were a combination of bus and lorry, with narrow wooden benches stretching the width of the cab, behind the driver, the rest of the space taken up with merchandise of every sort from sheep fleeces, farm produce and, probably, opium plants, to live chickens and goats.

There wasn't always a clear demarcation between passenger and cargo space and one was just as likely to find oneself in the rear sitting atop a pile of sacks, as alongside the beturbaned driver; sometimes as many as seven passengers would cram in, either side of him. Fortunately there was little need for him to search for the gear lever for the road seemed to stretch on endlessly and, apart from the odd Russian jeep, there was practically no other traffic.

We reached Kabul after several days of travelling like this. The Afghan capital is much nearer the Pakistan

frontier than the Iranian one, and there was quite heavy traffic down the Latterban and Khyber Passes to Peshawar, a town I have always associated with Kipling and his tales of the North West Frontier. Peshawar was still a pretty wild sort of place, with tribesmen striding around with rifles slung across their shoulders and long, curved knives stuck in their belts, but also white-uniformed traffic policemen with pith helmets directing camel trains, the twice-weekly little American-built International school bus which did the journey from Kabul and was used by tourists, Leyland Titan double-deckers and Bedford single-deckers and lorries. The bodies on these were locally built and were wonderfully ornate both inside and out, with vivid purple, orange or viridian shiny-plastic upholstery and holy Moslem pictures fixed in the windscreens, which were often bordered by imitation lace, and elaborate exterior patterns.

Six months later I did the journey again, out from England, this time driving an ex-military Bedford lorry over the snow-covered mountains of northern Turkey and then through Iran and Afghanistan to Pakistan, India and Kathmandu, the capital of Nepal. Although the final stretch of the journey, through the foothills of the Himalayas, was only 80 miles from the Indian border, such were the gradients that we did not reach our destination until the following afternoon.

Left:
The author and friends wash the Maudslay at Isfahan, Iran.

Top:
In August 1967 a Harrington-bodied AEC Reliance of Overlanders is washed ready for its journey east. Note the then-fashionable 'flower power' decor on the boot door.

Above:
Street Called Straight in Damascus.

Above:
At the head of the Khyber Pass, ornately-decorated Pakistani Bedfords stand at the Afghan border.

Left:
It might look like a truck, but this rugged Mack provided the bus service from Meshed to Herat.

Right:
In Peshawar in 1967 a Leyland Titan stands out in traffic made up otherwise of motorised and horse-drawn rickshaws.

The road, the Rajpath, had only recently been completed and climbed from a little above sea level to 8,000ft at its highest point. It was one of the hairiest drives I have ever had, as I eased around hairpin bends just wide enough for one vehicle, with a sheer rock face on one side and a drop of several thousand feet on the other. Whenever there were passing places we seemed to come across an Indian-owned bus, usually with a Sikh in charge, which either overtook us or shot off in the opposite direction at terrifying speed. During our 10-day stay in Kathmandu, one bus did go over the edge with fatal results; the other operators put notices in the newspaper, obviously already prepared for what was a fairly routine situation, to the effect that as far as they were concerned services were continuing as normal.

Until the opening of the Rajpath, the only means of reaching Kathmandu had been either on foot, by ex-US Air Force DC-3 (a flight not to be taken lightly), or by an aerial ropeway which looped up and down the mountains. This latter conveyed nearly all the merchandise needed in the capital and included motor vehicles in knocked-down form. On arrival the parts were removed from their packing-cases and reassembled. Thus a number of wonderfully venerable vehicles still made their stately way around Kathmandu, including several small school buses dating from the late 1920s and early 1930s.

I was reminded in some ways of those days in Nepal, more than 35 years ago, when I visited Cambodia in 1999. We flew into Phnom Penh from Bangkok, selected one of the several taxis desperate for our custom, and settled into the Indo-Chine hotel overlooking the Mekong River. Modern motor traffic seemed conspicuous by its absence. The civil war, following on from the horrors of the Pol Pot and Khmer Rouge regimes and the spilling over of the Vietnam War, had ended less than two years earlier; the infrastructure of the country had virtually collapsed.

Of Cambodian buses I can tell you very little, for Phnom Penh, the country's capital, possessed none. There was simply no public transport. Can you imagine such a thing? You could have an elephant ride around a recently-restored temple, the few taxis were linked to hotels, and the railway station was deserted save for beggars, whilst the tens of thousands of land mines were being cleared from the country's railway system. One simply walked or hitched a lift on the back of a motor cycle. A French fabric-dealer we met, visiting from Vietnam, told us that there were buses which ran between the capital and provincial cities, but they could not be relied upon owing to the state of the roads and the demolished bridges, whilst another European, a Belgian

hotel-owner in Siem Reap, said that there were none at all and that communications were worse than in the 1930s, though better than they had been when he had arrived with the UN in 1995.

I did see a few minibuses, and we hired one ourselves to visit Ankor Wat, but the locals appeared to hitch lifts in, or on, anything available. Twenty or more might squeeze themselves into the back of an Isuzu pick-up, and I saw a huge, battered six-wheel truck arrive from the country loaded with assorted goods piled higher than a double-deck bus, with, perched on top, some dozen or so passengers clinging to the ropes. They would have needed to cling very hard, for the rural roads consisted mostly of deep potholes joined by slightly less deep potholes.

The contrast with neighbouring Thailand could hardly have been greater. Never having been colonised by a European power, and having kept clear of the Indo-China and Vietnam conflicts, it is a country which has very much gone its own way, blessed with a hot, damp climate which enables it to grow fruit and cereals in glorious abundance. It has been selective in who it has approached to provide its transport infrastructure — USA and Europe to a degree, but primarily Japan and South Korea.

Right:
A Mercedes speeds along the Rajpath in 1967.

Below:
Late-1960s Nepal was home to ancient 1930s school buses.

It is in bad taste to make fun of those who speak English less than perfectly, especially when as a nation we tend to be worse than anyone else at learning other languages. But that won't stop me. Just as yesterday I had declined an offer in Bangkok to take a 'boat tip', so today I let go by a bus emblazoned with the slogan 'King Off the Road'. Thais are a gentle and forgiving people but I wouldn't say their buses totally reflect these national characteristics. They are prone to outbursts of sudden, frenzied action, and can be extremely noisy. On the positive side they are possibly the most colourful in the world.

I am writing this in Nakon Pathom, 40km west of Bangkok, having made several bus journeys around town. On one, the bus was so packed that the conductress could only reach a small proportion of the passengers. Speaking zilch Thai, I held up four fingers to indicate how many tickets I wanted and proffered 40 baht (about 70p) for the 15-minute journey. I received no change, but a ticket of such length that I suspect I paid for everyone on the bus.

Bangkok is notorious for its gridlocked rush hours, when it becomes quicker — if not particularly healthy — to walk. City buses, owned by the local authority, are divided into air-conditioned and non-air-conditioned, and priced and liveried accordingly. There are also many private operators, which mostly use green-painted minibuses, but the authority, as it upgrades its own services and with its long-overdue monorail system coming into use, intends to outlaw them.

The provincial road network is extensive; speeds can be high — too high sometimes — with a fair amount of dual carriageway. The Buddhist temples which dominate the country often look like Disney-inspired fantasies, unreal in their gold-covered opulence, and something of this delight in fantastically-rich colour schemes inspires the designers of private coach liveries. Consider the dull uniformity of Britain's NBC years and then think of the opposite extreme and you will have a good idea of what a privately-owned Thai coach can look like.

British coach liveries have become more adventurous of late, but not necessarily better, for too many are designed by amateurs with no overall understanding of shape, colour and pattern, and the result is timid, half-hearted and ugly. The best of the Thai liveries exhibit terrific pizzazz, a whoomph, a vitality which, in my experience, is unique. There is often a haphazard, sometimes comical, sometimes effective mixture of Thai and Western script. Any combination of colours is acceptable. The shapes are rather less dramatic, the bodywork being either of European or Far Eastern construction, the chassis of Volvo, Mercedes, MAN or Japanese or South Korean make.

As in most countries there is a distinction between buses and coaches. Most Westerners are likely to travel

on the efficient National coach network, very like National Express, covering the entire country. The coaches are air-conditioned and painted in a relatively restrained blue and white livery, often with an orange stripe. These cover journeys of anything from 40 to over 1,000km.

The route I know best is the 997, which operates out of Bangkok's Southern Bus & Coach station — an enormous, sprawling affair, although dwarfed by the five-storey Northern one. The 997 runs every 10 minutes to and from Nakon Pathom, Thailand's oldest city, famous for its Chedi — a vast temple in the heart of the city, where Buddhism first reached Thailand (or Siam, as it was called until around 50 years ago). Each coach has its route-number painted on the side, and also its running-number, London Transport-style, although in much bigger numerals — which are fortunately in Arabic numerals and therefore easy enough for Westerners to understand. Most coaches carry 'Bangkok-Nakon Pathom' on their sides in both English and Thai lettering.

Thais are desperate to learn English and to practise it at every opportunity, so you are sure of a welcome if you are prepared to be patient with the accent. At the Bangkok terminus you book your ticket at an office set aside exclusively for this route — other frequent routes have similar facilities — and you are given a ticket printed with the coach running-number and your seat number. It all works with great efficiency. You enter at the front, climb three quite steep steps — no low-floor mollycoddling — pass the engine-cover and find your place.

Every coach has a uniformed conductress. Thais love uniforms and dressing up and it is easy to mistake

university students for sixth-formers, for they all wear white blouses or shirts and grey or black skirts or trousers. It was the great sports weekend at the college where my son lectures. 'What do you think of the state of the field in the stadium?' he asked. 'Not too wonderful,' I replied. 'Exactly,' he said. 'It's not what happens on the sports field that counts, it's getting to be in one of the cheerleading teams. They'll spend months on their costumes but probably won't have a clue who won the match.'

Back to your coach. Your pale-blue-uniformed conductress will check your seat number and, later on, may come around with iced water. But don't ask her to turn off the video mounted above the driver at the front of the coach. If you are very lucky you may be treated to an episode of a Thai soap. These seem to be much along the lines of their Australian or British equivalents, the cast

Left:
Modern-day Bangkok, with non-air-conditioned city buses.

Inset (left):
Among the modern coaches running in Thailand is this unusual double-decker.

Above:
'Room for one more inside...!' Perhaps not. A Thai schoolbus shows an attitude to passenger safety which would give any UK legislator a heart-attack.

consisting of Thai actors and actresses trying to look as much like Westerners as possible, and real Westerners who seem to have been cast on account of nil acting ability. (My son starred in a Range Rover commercial even though he hadn't got a driving licence. He was well paid but has never acted before or since and refused to tell his mother and me when it was on, so we never got to see it.)

My more recent journeys in Asia had convinced me that the British bus and coach industry had given up trying to penetrate the Far Eastern market — although I should say I've not yet visited Hong Kong or Singapore. However, a visit to Malaysia in 1997 turned out to contain some pleasant surprises. We travelled from Penang to the Cameron Highlands in a Mercedes coach with a locally-built body. The winding journey up through the hills towards our destination brought back memories of the Rajpath. Whilst not so precipitous or high, it was spectacular enough and made more interesting (if that is the word) by the driver, who spent much of the journey in animated conversation with a passenger, often turning round to give him his full attention as he swung around the sharp bends, shouting above the roar of the engine.

The Cameron Highlands were pleasantly cool after the intense heat at sea level. The local bus company called itself 'Regent' and possessed a fleet of buses distinctly long in the tooth, which, although mostly the inevitable Mercedes, made one wonder if their predecessors might have been AEC Regals; Malaya was, of course, part of the British Empire, and AECs and Leylands had been familiar sights. Land Rovers were still popular and one came across the odd Morris Minor. The Cameron Highlands are famous for their tea, and we visited a

processing plant where the machinery had been imported from Belfast in the 1930s. I watched one of the elderly Regent buses winding its way up the steep hillside past Bangladeshis picking tea — a scene straight out of a Somerset Maugham novel.

Another air-conditioned Mercedes brought us to Kuala Lumpur, a city with plenty of style, a cricket ground in its heart, some handsome colonial architecture, a fantastical extravaganza of a railway station which must rank in the world's top ten, the tallest building in the world, some fine modern buildings inspired by traditional designs, and several British-built steam engines in the National Museum.

I was still reflecting wistfully on the decline of the British bus industry when what should heave into view but a Dennis Dart. I saw several more Dennises but these were merely a taster, for I quickly became aware of a very familiar shape, none other than the Optare MetroRider. My local company, Wilts & Dorset, sends them past my front door, although admittedly not air-conditioned. Kuala Lumpur had dozens of them, painted in an attractive pale grey and purple livery and lettered 'Intrakota'. You may imagine my delight at coming across these Leeds-designed vehicles — by a curious coincidence the preserved steam engines had been built by Kitson's of Leeds — almost on the equator.

So all ye of little faith (which included me) take heart, for there is clearly still a healthy future for the British bus in Asia.

Optare is one of a number of British bus manufacturers active in the Far East. This is a MetroRider – known locally as a Pekan Rider – in Kuala Lumpur.

ORKNEY
OVERTURE

Over the years, Roy Marshall has been a regular visitor to the Orkney Isles, which, though they start barely 10 miles from the Scottish mainland, are only occasionally visited by transport photographers.

Below:
Small buses were the standard fare on most Scottish islands, often as much to satisfy weight restrictions as to cope with narrow roads. Although it looks like a typical postwar Bedford OB, this is in fact a wartime OWB which had been rebodied by Duple. In 1964 it was being operated by Firth between Stromness and Kirkwall.

Inset:
An OWB with typical Duple utility body which was being operated by Loughton of Deerness in 1957. Loughton ran the Deerness-Kirkwall service from 1920 to 1977.

Above:
A more modern Bedford/Duple combination owned by Harvey of Evie and used on a service linking Evie with Kirkwall; this is another 1964 view. Harvey gave up the route in 1972.

Right:
Nicolson of Kirkwall used an unusual dark blue and maroon livery and in 1957 was operating this Plaxton-bodied Commer Avenger which had been bought new — note the local BS registration mark. Nicolson's business was taken over by Peace of Kirkwall in 1963.

Above:

Spence of St Margaret's Hope, on South Ronaldsay, introduced a service to Kirkwall in 1945, taking advantage of the new Churchill barriers which created direct road links between some of the southern islands. In 1957 Spence was running this 1937 Tiger TS7 with Alexander body which was still in the two-tone blue livery of previous owner W. Alexander & Sons. It was withdrawn in 1959.

Below:

Beneath this bizarre early-1950s KW body lies a 1938 Albion Valkyrie chassis. It was operated by Tait & Park of Stromness. KW was based in Blackpool and the Valkyrie came to Orkney from Dodds Coaches of Troon.

Right:
The garage of Wishart of Stromness provides the backdrop for this Bedford OB which Wishart used on a service to Kirkwall. Note the Austin Devon alongside.

Below:
Peace grew to become one of the big names in Orkney transport. A Churchill-bodied Austin, which had been new in 1951 to Macrae & Dick of Inverness, stands outside the company's Kirkwall office in 1964. It came to Orkney via Highland Omnibuses.

Below:
Another acquisition from the Scottish mainland was this AEC Regal II with Duple body. New to Scottish Omnibuses in 1946, it was bought by Peace in 1962 and served the company for five years.

ORKNEY
OVERTURE

Below:
More mundane vehicles have served Orkney, and this Plaxton-bodied Bedford is typical of the Peace coach fleet in the 1970s. The Peace operation, with 30 coaches, sold out to Inverness-based Rapson in the autumn of 1999.

Below:
Unusual vehicles do survive. The short Plaxton body, small wheels and rear-mounted engine signal that this is no run-of-the-mill coach despite its relatively modern E-prefix registration. Operating for Rosie of Evie in the summer of 1999, it has a rare Ward chassis. Rosie was bought by the Rapson group in September 1999.

FORTY YEARS OF TOURING

Geoff Mills looks back at 40 years of organising tours from Colchester for the PSV Circle.

Above:
The very first enthusiasts' tour in Colchester — in April 1960 — used a Corporation Guy Arab II with Gardner 5LW engine and Strachans body. New in 1944, it was withdrawn in December 1960.

Left:
Ten years later, three Massey-bodied Regent IIIs are lined up during a tour. These were 6812A models with 7.7-litre engines and crash gearboxes.

It all began in early 1960 when the last of Colchester Corporation's Guy Arabs with utility bodies were due for final withdrawal after over 15 years' faithful service. A town tour was devised using as many roads as possible within the borough which were not normally served by Corporation-owned buses.

Since that time, almost every type of borough bus has been given a fond farewell by local enthusiasts. These have included Bristol K6As in May 1964, Massey-bodied Regent IIs in December 1965, the unique Massey-bodied Crossley in September 1967, Daimler/Roberts in September 1968 (using the much-publicised No 4, recently extensively restored), AEC Regent IIIs in October 1970, Leyland PD2s (tin-front) with Massey bodywork in December 1971, Regent Vs in December 1973, ex-Leicester Reliances in February 1975 followed by ex-Salford Reliances in June of the same year, Bristol REs in March 1988, Metroriders in April 1990 and the last of the ECW-bodied Atlanteans still in Colchester Borough Transport livery (but in Arriva Colchester ownership) in December 1999.

Over the span of time other gems from a wide variety of operators have been sampled. One perpetual favourite was Norfolk's of Nayland. Vehicles supplied by Norfolk's have included a Leyland Cheetah/Alexander (in 1963), AEC Regal IV/Whitson (1966), ex-St Helens RT (1966), a normal-control Austin/Mann Egerton to celebrate 25 tours by the PSV Circle from Colchester in April 1968, an ex-Oxford Regent III with stylish Park Royal bodywork (1972) which later returned home for preservation, a former Bolton Regent V (1980), an ex-Reading Jumbo VR (1985) and a unique open-top AEC Renown (1989).

Not only have most of the vehicles utilised disappeared from the local scene, but so too have a vast number of the operators which so kindly provided the enthusiast fraternity with great days out at very reasonable rates. One such was Everson's of Wix (later Dovercourt) with a Leyland-Beadle rebuilt from a Birch Bros double-decker, a superb AEC Regal III/Duple new to Greenslades and a weird Austin K4 with 14-seat Plaxton body. Another was Vines of Great Bromley, whose vehicles over the years included various AECs and one of those strange ex-Aldershot & District Dennis Falcons with Strachans body.

Osborne's of Tollesbury contributed generously to our strange requests with an ex-London Transport private hire RF (later preserved), an RT, an ex-demonstration AEC Renown and other second-hand double-deckers including a former Eastern National FLF, and an ex-Tayside Fleetline and VRT, both with Alexander bodies.

Adventures have been many, disasters relatively few. On the return from Southend after some 12 hours of continuous rain a Roberts-bodied Daimler had to plough through water over 2ft deep, not all of which stayed on the outside of the bus. Then there was the ex-Salford Reliance which had serious charging problems to the extent that the lighting got increasingly dim as the daylight started to fade.

The ex-demonstration Renown blew a hole in the exhaust system — ingeniously repaired by a fitter using flattened discarded drinks cans retrieved from a litter bin. A rare Thurgood-bodied Bedford OB developed fuel starvation problems before it reached the borough boundary and was unceremoniously pushed into an unmade road where a sign ominously warned: Dumping of Rubbish Prohibited.

An ex-Timpson Harrington-bodied Reliance from the same operator lived up to the reputation of the AEC 470 engine for boiling. At an operator with which we had a pre-arranged visit, it was abandoned when we received the kind offer of a trusty Bristol LHL with a reliable Leyland 401 engine. Another Bristol fared less well — an ex-Epsom Coaches LHS. It developed a serious rumbling noise which turned out to be a loose bolt in the universal joint — and was replaced during the tour by a Perkins-engined Seddon. On a later trip in the same Bristol, with a subsequent owner, it suffered clutch failure.

Since 1969 there have been sufficient members with PSV driver's licences to hire vehicles on a self-drive basis, which has increased the enjoyment and decreased the cost.

By the close of 1999 some 195 day trips had been successfully operated for Colchester meetings of the PSV Circle, using over 350 vehicles — and the only member to have been on every venture is the organiser.

In 1971 this restored Bristol LS5G, new to United Auto but latterly owned by Hedingham & District, overheated. It was heading to an event at Pakenham Mill and had to be towed back to Ixworth by the unusual Seddon.

Above:
A Kelvedon Coaches Reliance — complete with PSV Circle tour board in the windscreen in this view in Colchester's High Street — managed just 40 miles before overheating and being replaced by a Bristol LH.

Below:
A smart ex-Eastern National FLF running for Sutton's of Clacton-on-Sea meets up with a former shed-mate at Southchurch Park, Southend, in the summer of 1978. Both buses were new in 1960; the vehicle on the right had been converted to a driver trainer by Eastern National.

Above:
This neat LHS, also in the High Street, developed a strange rumbling noise when a bolt in the universal joint started working loose in 1983...

Right:
... and five years later, with a new owner, later style of front panel and a cherished number-plate, it suffered clutch failure, but could be driven home, cautiously.

Left:
In 1989 this unique Marshall-bodied Bedford YRT of Hedingham was used for a trip to the Cambus rally at Peterborough. The battery had to be disconnected when a wiring loom began to smoke. Coincidentally, fire would destroy the Bedford in 1999.

Below:
In April 1990 a Colchester Metrorider, newly repainted in white, grey and blue, made its first outing on a PSV Circle tour. It is seen at West Thurrock, alongside one of three Metroriders operated by Harris Bus. Colchester had five Metroriders, all of which were sold to Strathclyde Buses after just three years in service.

Right:
A special quest? This unusual bus was a Quest 80 with Locomotors body, operated by Smith's of Buntingford and seen on a PSV Circle tour at Braughing, Hertfordshire, in 1990. It had been new to Ralph's of Langley for use at Heathrow Airport, hence the offside door. Note the Ford truck grille — the Quest 80 was Ford-powered.

Right:
Another rare Quest. This 1987 coach has 37-seat Jonckheere bodywork and was new to Roberts Coaches of Plymouth. It was owned by Graham's of Kelvedon when used for a tour from Colchester in 1991.

Below:
A farewell to Colchester's Bristol REs in March 1988 involved visiting other RE operators in the area. The Colchester bus is flanked by two ex-West Yorkshire buses owned by Norfolk's of Nayland.

Above:

Plaxton's unusual Mini Supreme was sampled on a 1992 trip, using this coach owned by Felix of Long Melford. It was a 25-seater based on a Mercedes-Benz L608D chassis and had been new to The Londoners.

Above:

While Leyland was developing its rear-engined Royal Tiger, an enterprising Leeds operator, Independent Coachways, was building a Leopard with a rear-mounted engine using parts from two older Leopard chassis, one C-registered, the other J-registered. Plaxton fitted a Supreme IV body to this unique chassis in 1981. By 1992 it was owned by Lewis of Bury St Edmunds, and had acquired a Paramount front panel.

Above:
...By 1993 it had been bought by Graham's of Kelvedon, and repainted and retrimmed. It is seen at that year's Southend bus rally.

THE YELLOW DOG AND THE FLOATING BRIDGE

Robert E. Jowitt, with the usual diversions off the regular routes, follows the fortunes of Southampton Corporation buses for 40 years, from the last trams to the Routemaster foray.

'We must ride on a knifeboard,' said my father. 'This will be our last chance, ever!' This was in 1948 or 1949, the town was Southampton, and we made a special excursion for the purpose from our home in Winchester. Thus my first experience of Southampton Corporation Transport was travelling on a knifeboard-seat open-top tram — the last of this breed extant, and about to be swept into oblivion.

If the term 'tram' is coming back into the English language in this new millennium and 'open-top' is pretty familiar in tourist transport today, the other qualifying adjective, 'knifeboard-seat', is perhaps sufficiently Victorian to require some explanation. A knifeboard was a common device in 19th century kitchens for the sharpening of knives, and a knifeboard seat was a back-to-back bench placed longitudinally along the top deck of an electric tram (with the upright base for the trolleypole sticking up out of the middle of it), which appeared to Victorian eyes to bear some resemblance to the household contraption. . . until such time as it occurred to tramway operators that more passengers could be carried on rows of cross-wise seats.

Without wallowing further in this matter — for those who wish to know more can find ample literature on the subject — I must say that, while I doubtless duly appreciated the charms of the knifeboard, we sampled other sorts of tram too; I remember, even at the tender age of five or six, actually liking rather better the closed-in-top cars with open balconies at the ends, which may be the reason why this type has remained my favourite sort of double-deck tram ever since.

Then the whole war-weary outfit was scrapped, except for a number of the newest cars which were snapped up by Leeds as second-hand bargains and one knifeboard tram which was saved and, after sitting in the rain at Beaulieu Motor Museum for some years, eventually rose again to travel the

rails at Crich. Meanwhile my father's next pilgrimage with me was to what was known as the 'tramatorium', a term of stunning originality applied at that date, I believe, to almost every scrapyard in tram-scrapping cities in Britain. This example lay near Northam, and we emerged from it with a destination box purchased for the princely sum, if I recall correctly, of half a crown (or 12½p). I think as I look at it now — it has hung on my wall (in my youth by my bed and, more recently, in my study) ever since — that it is probably a side-window box. At moments in my life when I fancied girls called Mary or Shirley I turned the blind to DOCKS VIA ST MARY'S or SHIRLEY; at other times I have contented myself with DOCKS VIA HIGH ST, BITTERNE TRIANGLE, SPECIAL, FLOATING BRIDGE . . .

Ten years old but immaculate, this 1950 Guy Arab — taking a corner in sporting style, determined not to be overtaken by the MG — is typical of the Southampton fleet in the decade following the last tram.

Some of the destinations might prove as incomprehensible to present-day citizens of Southampton as the term 'knifeboard', due to pedestrian zones, changes in transport politics, and the fact that Southampton has altered — I hesitate to use the word 'sunk' in a nautical connection and lest it be deemed a denigration — from a major transatlantic and cross-Channel port to a container terminal. . . and of course you can still catch a ferryboat to the Isle of Wight or a

Above:
Probably considered beautiful now, the Park Royal PD2s appeared uncompromisingly square — and excessively over-painted in dark red — when new in 1961. 305 is seen at Portswood, not far up the road from the Yellow Dog.

Above right:
Both bodies are by Park Royal, but with minimal cream relief and no rear destination display, 1961 Leyland PD2 304 lacks the elegance of 1949 Guy Arab 165.

Right:
By 1972 the Leyland PD2s had been repainted with more cream, as here on 312, doing much to improve their appearance.

smaller ferryboat to Hythe, which still boasts a 2ft-gauge electric tram along its pier.

If Hythe Pier adhered faithfully to electric traction, Southampton Corporation placed its faith in a fleet of Park Royal-bodied Guy Arabs, and not unreasonably, for they gave many years' good service and, if you could accept them at all as disposers of trams, were handsome vehicles besides. The biggest batch, starting at fleet number 104, was of just over 50 vehicles arriving for obvious 'un-tramming' reasons in 1948, but there had been small deliveries of Guy Arabs before that (some subsequently converted to open-top). Roughly 100 more had arrived by 1954, to serve new estates which were springing up beyond the erstwhile tram termini on allotment gardens and empty heaths as the vegetables and gorse bushes had flourished before them.

One of the Guy buses achieved some notoriety as being guinea-pig for Cave-Brown-Cave ventilator experiments, a feature which in modified form soon became standard on a great number of Bristol Lodekkas. Another member of the Cave-Brown-Cave family, in the abbreviated form of Paul Cave, was responsible for the famous and delightful *Hampshire Magazine*, with occasional articles over the past 30 years by Robert E. Jowitt following in the footsteps of his father and mother.

Setting aside family pride (as it says you must, in Gilbert and Sullivan's *The Mikado*), I have to admit that I would have been unaware of the existence of the Cave-Brown-Cave guinea-pig — though, unlike later Lodekka versions, the ventilator was huge and went right across the front above the cab — had it not been brought to my attention by a more clued-up bus-spotting acquaintance. This same worthy chap also tried to bring my attention to bear on sundry Southampton single-deckers (which were always few and far between because only one route had a low bridge, under the main line north of Swaythling), but in this he was largely unsuccessful, for I wasn't very interested in buses anyway (give me a tram any day). Southampton's principal allure lay in the street known as Above Bar, because this, despite the dreadful architecture (devastating air raids in 1940, audible a dozen miles away, destroyed a major portion of the city centre and the essays in rebuilding were among the most dreary post-Blitz specimens in Britain) was the busiest street in the city (whatever merits the High Street may once have had, the demographic changes following the war had reduced it to a dingy purlieu) and accordingly was thriving with lovely girls.

The Bar, incidentally, had nothing to do with pubs; it was the mediæval Bargate and the open-top trams had to creep through it with awful warnings from the conductors to upper-deck passengers. Later, the closed-top cars had to be built to special, squat dimensions to fit through, and thus such of these as escaped to Leeds looked very dumpy among their taller, northern sisters. The Bargate had been bypassed by the time the Guy Arabs arrived — otherwise these might have appeared in quasi-East Yorkshire form.

Nevertheless, the Guy Arabs were constantly there as a background to all these girls, and the main background at that; the single-deckers scarcely appeared in this area — I ignored them then, and I have ignored Southampton single-deckers ever since. The Guy Arabs, if you could accept buses in formerly tram-ridden streets, were the souls of the streets of Southampton, and seemed as if they would last for ever.

Sadly, I cannot include photos of Sue with whom — greatly daring and as a consequence of snapshooting her on the pavements — I managed to strike an acquaintance; the snapshots didn't include Guy Arabs either. Sue came with me to the pleasures of the Easter Fair on the Common, and as she lived in Woolston, she must needs have walked on and off the Floating Bridge every time she came into Southampton. The Floating Bridge was a chain ferry of magnificent bulk, crossing the River Itchen in antiquated splendour, surviving long after you might have thought it could have done, and in fact until 1977, whereafter it was replaced by a rather exciting, steeply-graded bridge which present-day buses attack with panache; but until the ferry passed away it was obviously an important terminus for buses as much as for the trams before them.

Sue, with no more than the fondness a fairground ride allows, was gone far, far sooner, and suddenly the Guy Arabs were going too. Attentive readers of *Buses Yearbook* may recall that, in an article which appeared two or three years ago dealing with Bath, I managed to include a digression on my youth when I played at being a *Dolce Vita*-type photographer taking flash shots of bright young things in Winchester society and how, being at that moment girl-less, I was acting as chauffeur in a Ford Prefect to my sister and her sweetheart after a late-evening party; encountering an SCT Guy

Arab being driven away to (presumably) some northern scrapyard, I had set off in pursuit in what I deemed quite *Dolce Vita* manner to attempt to flash-photo it on the end of the film which had been devoted to cathedral-city-gilded youth, the photos of Guy Arab being, alas, undoubtedly less successful. My sister's boyfriend considered the pursuit highly successful, though he had little or no interest in Guys or indeed any buses. Had I been with a girl in the back of a Prefect I might not have, for that matter.

A bit later on, coming up from the depths of the Yellow Dog with Carol for necessary gasps of air, I saw the replacements for the Guys; being with Carol, even if sitting on the pavement rather than an automobile back seat, I didn't pay them much attention either. Carol was not in truth a Southampton girl — she was a Bournemouth girl and proud of it, and her portrait has appeared more than once in my pages in *Buses Annual* and *Yearbook* with attendant trolleybuses — but she

frequently graced the floor of the Yellow Dog, skip-jiving wildly with me to Kid Martyn's Band or Lew Hird with Pamela the Australian trumpet-player or other splendid New Orleans jazz bands blasting forth glorious traditional classics such as 'High Society', 'Just a Little While to Stay Here', and 'Maryland, my Maryland'.

The Yellow Dog was a jazz club in the cellar of an alehouse — I regret to say I forget its name — on the Bevois Valley Road, or perhaps, more properly, Bevois Hill on the corner where Dukes Road turned off towards what had once been the tramatorium. Just occasionally, when the place became altogether too airless, the otherwise blacked-out windows were opened to afford a view of the site of the tramatorium and the main line beyond, with once the vision of an all-Pullman boat express behind a Bulleid Pacific beating northwards. Normally, breathlessness prevailed, along with some degree of darkness, for the walls were largely painted black. There was, however, a notable mural with a likeness of the yellow dog and the immortal words, slightly misquoted, from Edward Fitzgerald's 'Rubaiyat of Omar Khayyam':

A loaf of bread, a flask of wine, and thee beside me in the wilderness. . .

followed by the slightly less immortal but equally unforgettable line:

And soon I'll be fat, drunk, and in trouble.

Well, Carol and I never had loaves of bread or flasks of wine at the Yellow Dog, we had pints of beer, and in coming up frequently to fetch them from the bar and, as I have said, seeking air outside, we saw the new generation charging up Bevois Hill for Portswood and Swaythling or down the hill for

the centre. The new generation were still half-cab, but they were all what I would call tin-front, and looked fatter and less elegant than the Guys. For all I know, they may have been wider; I wasn't interested in finding out then, with 'Over in the Gloryland' pounding in my head, and I have never had occasion to find out since. Some of them, at least at their earliest appearance, looked all the newer (and, arguably, considerably the worse) for what I seem to remember as an overall unrelieved maroonish red. I must suppose that other people besides me found this unpleasant for, while I never said anything about it, except perhaps to Carol, *en passant*, as it were, while the buses were *en passant* the Yellow Dog, the livery was in due course modified to contain cream in suitable places, more in the style of the Guys.

Anyway, the new generation consisted of a dozen Leyland PD2/27s, with perforated-slot tin-front, 10 AEC Regent Vs with typical AEC front, and a further 20 PD2A/27s with 'juke-box' glass-fibre front, and all with

Park Royal bodies. . . like the Guys, but I still maintain they looked broader. This lot were numbered from 301 up, though an ancient Prince Marshall and Basil Kennedy *abc* suggests the first 12 were going to be 259-270. I didn't have the *abc* in my pocket at the Yellow Dog, so I don't know if these numbers saw the light of day; at all events, the first Titan received the number-plate 301 TR while the first Regent V was 313 AOW with the rest of the Regent Vs and the next lot of PD2As following on from there.

The new blood by no means entirely ousted the Guys, for there were still over 100 in the fleet by the time I had foolishly allowed Carol and the Yellow Dog to be torn out of my life; no wonder I thought the Guys looked fit to last for ever! Meanwhile, the Corporation Transport — like my life — was taking a new direction, or at least partly. The next 60 buses, starting at 343, were AEC Regent Vs and they were all bodied by East Lancs, or, in some cases, in East Lancs fashion by Neepsend. Furthermore, from 373 they were semi-automatic and also 30ft rather than 27ft 6in long, but with the increased length only four extra seats were added, bringing the total to 70 and representing thus a high degree of comfort for the passenger.

While the first of the East Lancs buses, 343, was registered 363 FCR, from 358 they started into B and then C, D, E and F suffixes, and a bit incoherently besides if you choose to check up on a fleet list, with, just to quote a few in order, BTR 358-61B, then BOW 502C, BTR 363B, BOW 501C, BTR 365B, BOW 503C, BTR 367B, then BOW 504C, and so on with 372 being BOW 508C, whereafter 373 was FOW 378D, 374-80 were HCR 131-7D. Reason prevailed for a spell from 381 with JCR 381E, and was lost again on the last 10 with 393-402 becoming KOW 901-10F.

At that date I paid scant attention to fleet lists, and occasional visits to Southampton for shopping or theatre or steam-train hunting seemed to reveal the situation as fairly *status quo*, or half-cab and open rear platform, even if perhaps there weren't any more Guys; until the date when, for diverse reasons, visits became more frequent and I became aware of a whole new scenario. If Southampton buses, as long as I had known them, had always been a remarkably standard fleet, first all Guy, then all new-look-front, now they were suddenly all Atlantean. Here and there a juke-box-front Leyland or, more frequently, a Regent V forced its familiar silhouette below those depressing Above Bar shoeboxes, but the new silhouette of front-entrance/rear-engine was more and more and more the silhouette of buses in Southampton until 1981 when the last Regent died; whereafter, in such bits of Above Bar as were still allowed to buses after pedestrianisation had banned them from much of it — in its rapidly-changing fashion parade from miniskirts through Vietnam combat suits and midi and maxi skirts and all sorts of other fashions back to miniskirts, while its architecture remained unchanged and dire, or, if changed, worse! — you could see queues of five or six identical Atlanteans and the fleet appeared as unified as it had in the all Guy Arab days.

But if you started to look twice it wasn't quite so simple. The Atlanteans came in six batches, or, if you choose to be particularly pernickety, 10 batches, between 1968 and 1981, starting with number 101 and reaching 276, and certainly in the six lots, if perhaps not in all 10, each delivery differed slightly from the one before — well, over 13 years it would, wouldn't it? — in such matters as the position, or absence, of ventilators and other similar trifles. You could spend hours — except that it was difficult because of the charms tripping by on the pavement — trying to spot the variations.

I do not propose to furnish details of them here — for there are several excellent publications on the subject — save only to say firstly that, of the second batch, one vehicle never arrived — the excellent publications give it as either 122 or 123 — because it was destroyed by fire at the East Lancs works, and secondly that the second half of the second batch (which might perhaps be described as the third batch) had number-plates starting at WOW 527J on fleet number 137. The lowest numbers of the WOW-J series were eagerly sought by owners of rakish sports cars; WOW 10J would sometimes park near my house in Winchester and be admired by its owner and his girlfriend while I, from a discreet distance, admired her; her name, incidentally, was Sue. As for the rest of the Atlantean number-plates, the earlier ones bore little or no likeness to the fleet numbers but from 202 onwards, with MCR 202R in 1977, they followed faithfully except for the freak of 217 and 219 which received respectively ORV 90 and 89S. All in all, however, if you did not trouble with number-plates and ventilators and if, as in my case, your eye was always more on Northam nymphs or Bitterne beauties, the degree of standardisation was stunning.

But then, if the clicking-clacking of some high-heeled shoes down some side street off Above Bar should cause you to look aside, you might come upon a whole world of different buses, or, indeed, if you went far enough along Above Bar you would see them cutting across it at right angles. Of course, the Hants & Dorset buses had always been there, tucked away in the background. Their bus station, nearly opposite the Civic Centre with its carillon playing 'O God Our Help in Ages Past' by Southampton's most famous citizen Isaac Watts, had been ceremonially opened by no less a dignitary than Sir Reginald Ford, Chairman of the Southern Area Traffic Commissioners, in 1933, to tidy up a story of earlier inadequate premises and halting places on the streets.

Far left:
315 was one of the first batch of AECs — 10 vehicles delivered in 1961/2, and the only Southampton Regents bodied by Park Royal. Jowitt at the time had little interest in this fact, and even less in the single-decker beyond. His attention in 1972 was plainly elsewhere. . .

Left:
390 was among the first set of 70-seat Regent V/East Lancs buses new in 1966. The tree-clad parks of the city centre are among Southampton's chief charms.

The Hants & Dorset buses themselves were no different from those I could see in Winchester when I lived in Winchester or those I could see in New Milton when I lived in New Milton — generally Bristols of one sort or another and mostly Ks and, later, Lodekkas, and

Top:
In 1978, whichever way you look at it, Regents and Titans can still be found among the Atlanteans. . .

Above:
. . . but five years later, in 1983, the Atlanteans have the streets to themselves.

Right:
Straying off the beaten track of Southampton Corporation buses, we visit the Hants & Dorset bus station in 1972 to find a 1955 Bristol LD6G with a yellow spot for Southampton depot above its fleet number.

not without a sprinkling of single-decks. These single-decks latterly included a number of RELLs which rather took my fancy and MW6G coaches converted to buses which took my fancy even more, including one painted blue which, if you wandered even further from Above Bar, could be discovered conveying passengers between the Central station and a relatively short-lived hovercraft crossing to Cowes, Isle of Wight. The double-deckers, as I have implied, I viewed as mundane, but the bus station itself, with its fading 1930s architectural grandeur and tacky tacked-on later excrescences and litter-strewn floor and splendid rows of parked buses and constant departures to unknown or unknowable corners of Hampshire, boasted a considerable (if dissolute) charm.

In the outer wilds of Southampton suburbia, before they reached their 'own' territory, the Hants & Dorset buses rivalled to some extent the efforts of the Corporation vehicles, or at least duplicated their routes, but, if I travelled not infrequently on the H&D 47 between Southampton and Winchester, I have no knowledge of what legal terms and conditions applied on these roads,

any more than I have any acquaintance with the Corporation buses on their outer extremities. No, I stayed always in the proximity of the fashion parade in the middle of town. And sometimes I have thought this was a mistake, as, for example, when I was called upon to judge the photographic competition of the Southampton University Transport Society, and felt bound to award a high place to a wonderful photograph of a Southampton Atlantean sliding sideways in frost and ice down a steep slope in the Far East somewhere beyond the Itchen. If I could remember who the photographer was I would beg the editor to reproduce the photograph here.

Unfortunately I can't, so neither can the editor, so we return to the city, and must now consider the impact of deregulation. From that dread date, even if, first of all, the Atlanteans battled on apparently unperturbed and as if likely to last for eternity like the Guys before them (and, in truth, with as little hope), new influences sprang at once to the fore. To sum it up briefly and not necessarily in chronological order (and it would require 80 rather than eight pages to cover the subject adequately) Hants & Dorset, after various transmogrifications such as Hampshire Bus — at which stage it had decorated the highways round Southampton with 10 ex-London DMS buses in red, white and blue with OUC and OJD registrations and fleet numbers 1917-26 — had finally succumbed to the blue, red and orange stripes of Stagecoach.

Upon these the previously entirely insular Southern Vectis from the Isle of Wight launched an attack under the name of Solent Blue Line — though the Solent is, like the Danube, more often a dirty grey, and whence the Solent Blue Line acquired the yellow which added the third part to the two-tone blue livery must remain a mystery; smart as it is, it does not reflect the sands of the Solent — and acquired the 47 from Southampton to Winchester and many other routes out of Southampton as well, following a brief, crazy passage when Stagecoach had allowed Southampton Corporation to operate the 47.

As I have said above, this chaos would require 80 pages of elucidation, and the main point is that ex-Southern Vectis VRs in the new livery began dangerously to threaten the territory of the cream-with-red-stripe livery of the Atlanteans — this reversal from Guy Arab colours, which I have so far forgotten to mention, had been applied since the Atlanteans first arrived — and, to counter the invasion, especially on the Shirley and Millbrook routes, Citybus, as the Corporation Transport was now known in up-to-date phraseology, tossed in a fleet of 15 ex-London Transport Routemasters, still in more-or-less London red, with the great attraction of conductors as in days of yore and no hanging about at bus stops.

Of these buses the oldest was RM564 (WLT 564) and the newest was RM2059 (ALM 59B), with various CLT and DYE and ALD-B and ALM-B in between. These

heroes of antiquity received fleet numbers at random, recorded as 402 to 415, except for WLT 820 which was allotted no number and presumably was cannibalised for spares; it might be supposed that this bus would otherwise have been 401, but the truth is that the RMs were joined by another veteran, namely Southampton's own 401 or the penultimate Regent, bearing the inscription of 'Southampton's last open-platform bus' which, I assume, it had borne when it was actually serving as such, before it was hidden away at the demise of the Regents some eight years previously.

While this invasion of rejuvenated pensioners might be regarded as a deregulation bonus, on the minus side Stagecoach sold out its Hants & Dorset bus station site, presumably for a fairly handsome mess of pottage, to skyscraper developers. Henceforth it sited its stops in the main streets as they had inconveniently been in the backward 1930s, along with such new interlopers as the republican-entitled People's Provincial, which was sending out elderly Leyland Nationals on to new routes far-flung from its former Gosport and Fareham territory in the distant southeast of Hampshire, and Wilts & Dorset, which from sharing one route from Salisbury with Hants & Dorset inconspicuously into a corner of the bus station began instead, in bright red and white with black lines, prominently to skirt the very walls of the Bargate.

The Routemasters made as pretty and almost as traditional a picture as the Regents before them, but I cannot answer for their fate — though I don't believe it was long before it fell — for in 1989, at the height of their re-incarnated glory, I moved 150 miles away to dabble in the buses of the Welsh Marches, and from that moment my acquaintance with Southampton buses effectively ceased.

When I returned, 10 years later, to take up residence in real Southern Vectis country — namely the Isle of Wight — the buses in Southampton were all inscribed 'First'. No Citybus, certainly no Corporation Transport, absolutely no RMs, and there were an awful lot of single-deckers which,

Left:
Eleven years later, in 1983, the line-up in the bus station is a generation newer and includes Bristol REs, VRs, LHs, Leyland Nationals and an ex-London DMS.

Above:
Southampton Corporation's answer to new rivals after deregulation was a fleet of ex-London RMs which, with conductors, had the merit of eliminating delays at bus stops. Here, in the shadow of Bargate, it almost looks like Piccadilly.

as I had never taken any interest in Southampton single-deckers, I did my best to ignore. Once or twice an Atlantean slunk almost apologetically on to the scene — undoubtedly one of the later vehicles with a number-plate to match its fleet number — and for a moment, amidst the cranes building even more new skyscrapers, though not yet demolishing the Above Bar disasters, I thought back to the days when Atlanteans shared the streets with Regents, and thus to when Regents chased Guy Arabs to the Floating Bridge, with Sue aboard, and when tin-front Leylands roared past the wild, hot joys of the Yellow Dog. *And thee beside me in the wilderness.* And in this wilderness of cranes with thee, Carol, long, long gone from beside me, I wondered whether someone would soon slap a listed building order on to the mess of Above Bar, which —

even if, only 50 years after it was built, it can hardly be said to have stood the test of time — is now as archaic as knifeboards had been when I first — and last — travelled on them.

Now I think I will go and find some old 45s, 'Maryland' and 'High Society', and while I am playing them I will turn my destination blind to FLOATING BRIDGE. . .

And Solent Blue Line's answer to the RM was the 'Conductor Bus', operating mostly on the very same streets.

TURNING *THE* CLOCK BACK

Bus preservation is such a well-established pastime that many old vehicles have now spent longer in retirement than they did in service. Michael Fowler turns the clock back some 30 years to illustrate vehicles which have entered preservation since the late 1960s.

Air-cooled engines were never common in British buses and this unusual Guy Arab III with a Ruston-Hornsby engine was in the ownership of the Lincolnshire Vintage Vehicle Society in 1969. This was in fact the vehicle's third engine; it had been an exhibit at the 1948 Commercial Motor Show with a Meadows unit, and for much of the 1950s ran with a Leyland engine. Guy built the body.

Also in LVVS ownership in 1969 was this unusual open-sided Bedford OB from the Lincolnshire Road Car fleet. It has a Duple body and had been acquired from Western National in 1960. It was used on a seafront service in Skegness.

Left:
On the Trans-Pennine run in 1969, a Durham District Bristol L leads two Southdown Leylands — a postwar Titan and a prewar Tiger — on the road between Shipley and Guisley.

Below:
Same spot, two years later, and a rare Daimler CD650 is followed by a Ford Anglia which was commonplace then but would now itself be a preservation candidate. The Daimler was one of four CD650s operated by Blue Bus of Willington and has lowbridge Willowbrook bodywork.

Top:
A sunny Sandtoft in September 1973. Two Bedford OBs flank a sales stand which is doing a roaring trade. Buses in the background include AEC Regents from West Bridgford, Huddersfield and York Pullman. A visitor in the foreground models the 1973 season anorak, suggesting the day was colder than it looks.

Above:
The 1972 Trans-Pennine makes its way through Otley with two early postwar municipal buses in view. The single-decker is a West Bromwich Daimler, the double-decker a Stockport PD2.

TURNINGTHE
CLOCK **BACK**

Above:
AEC Qs were never common at rallies, and this Green Line coach attracts its fair share of attention. New in 1935, it has a 37-seat BRCW body.

Right:
The unique Stalybridge, Hyde, Mossley & Dukinfield Atkinson double-decker climbs towards Otley on the 1974 Trans-Pennine run. It has a Northern Counties body and a Gardner engine.

Below right:
Same day, same spot, and a Bristol K from the Bristol fleet, with a Volkswagen preparing to overtake.

TURNING *THE* CLOCK **BACK**

Above:
The classic outline of a utility Guy Arab II which had been new to Swindon Corporation. It has highbridge Weymann bodywork. The Gardner-engined Arab I and II laid the foundations for some modest postwar sales success by Guy.

Below:
A 1951 AEC Regent III from Eastbourne Corporation positively glistens on the 1974 Trans-Pennine run. It has an East Lancs body which had been completed by Bruce Coachworks, and had been withdrawn by Eastbourne in 1971.

Below:
Sandtoft 1984, and one of the intriguing mirror-image AEC double-deckers
operated by Carris in Lisbon. The prominent bumper is a commentary on
Portuguese driving standards. Carris operated a substantial fleet of AECs, which
included Regal IIIs, Regent IIIs and Regent Vs.

TURNING *THE*
CLOCK **BACK**

SAVER SEVENTY-SEVEN

Oliver Howarth buys a ticket back to a Manchester of flares, Follyfoot and fondue. With photography by Roy Marshall.

The booking clerk behind the grille at Bury railway station smiled slightly when I asked for a platform ticket. Wondering why, I paid my 2p and received a grey slice of pasteboard entitling me to spend one hour on the platform. I was twelve and, having moved from Ladybank in Fife to Bury a few weeks earlier in that sweltering summer of '76, I was keen to pick up where my trainspotting had left off.

I soon saw why the clerk had smiled. Bury's trains differed somewhat from Ladybank's. No Deltics charging round the sharp bend of the station throat at 50mph; no thundering Brush Type 4-hauled Freightliners nor coal trains double-headed by Class 20s. Instead a Class 504 EMU came in, waited seven minutes and departed back to Manchester. There followed twenty-three minutes of nothing. The paint on the bench seat crackled slightly in the oppressive sunlight as I drew patterns in the dust with my toe. A second Class 504 came in and seven minutes later went out. There was nothing about the 504 to excite attention; it was the rail-borne equivalent of a Morris Marina, but not as thrilling.

Congealed by boredom I insisted on overstaying my legal time by four minutes (I believe the statute of limitations for this offence has expired by now, which is why I am able to confess this) in order to confirm my suspicions and yes, the first Class 504 returned. All trainspotting for the day was clearly over. I closed my *abc*, trudged out past the smirking ticket collector and into the hurly-burly of Bury. What a waste of 2p!

Outside, Bolton Street was fairly buzzing with traffic and I suddenly realised that all the buses were different. Every one was painted orange and white but they were all shapes and sizes and carried prominent numbers — stock numbers? The buses in Ladybank had been few and far between but here was a rich lode. Maybe I could spot them instead. I would be a pioneer, working in virgin territory — The First Bus Spotter.

A member of this batch was the first bus Oliver Howarth ever photographed — the print contained a lot of sky and one very blurred headlight and consequently the wise Mr Marshall has had to supply illustrations for this article. This vehicle, a Liverpool-style Atlantean, was new to Bury Corporation in 1963.

Well needless to say, it didn't work out like that. On a bookstall in Manchester's Piccadilly railway station I discovered the July 1976 issue of *Buses* and a little later, at the newsagency in Bolton's grubby Moor Lane bus station, I found the *Fleetbooks* for Greater Manchester and Lancashire & Cumbria. In the meantime I had built up my own designations and theories, but now I had real names and histories instead of my (much more imaginative) invented classifications. Mind you, I could never have dreamt up the name Atlantean. The reasons for all the different designs of bus now became clear — the GMT fleet was a concatenation of many smaller fleets, all of which had pursued different fleet policies and favoured different makes from year to year. And Bury was a melting pot for it all — what a fascinating place to be.

Bury, Gateway to Ramsbottom

To begin with, the Bury allocation of 108 vehicles (12 of them outstationed at Ramsbottom) had many visually-distinct types and several strangers in the ranks. Bury had in the 'fifties bought Weymann-bodied PD3s with a T-shaped destination blind arrangement favoured by the General Manager of the time, Mr Frank Thorpe — a blind arrangement originally used by Manchester Corporation on its 1933 to 1935 deliveries, when he had worked there. The last two had recently been withdrawn but were tucked away at the back of the depot and were still to be seen carrying L-plates.

The next purchase by Bury Corporation had been 'Lenny' (LEN 101), a Guy Wulfrunian, but that avenue had not been pursued and in 1963 a batch of 15 Atlanteans had arrived with MCW bodywork. These were basically to Liverpool Corporation's peaked and elegantly-chamfered design, disguised by the T-shaped blinds which looked better finished than Liverpool's idiosyncratic blind arrangement. In 1963 Mr Thorpe moved to Newport, but not before ordering another 15 double-deckers — Fleetlines this time and with Alexander's stylish highbridge bodywork complete with curved upper front screens and those T-shaped blinds. The stylish bodywork was, my parents tell me, a matter of civic pride in Bury. By the by, Mr Thorpe's first act in Newport was to order another 15 identical bodies, but on Atlantean chassis.

Inset (above right):
Bury's 1964 deliveries consisted of Fleetlines with Glasgow-style Alexander bodies. This one demonstrates the distinctive front end with a very large 'main' destination screen. Most operators would have crammed a route number and possibly an intermediate point into an aperture of this size but Bury preferred to use a single VERY BIG word.

Below:
Due to the large number of types and body styles purchased, Bury Corporation's fleet looked incoherent compared to those of surrounding operators. The 1965 deliveries were Sheffield-style Fleetlines bodied by East Lancs, with curved lower screens and flat upper screens — whereas the previous year's deliveries from Falkirk had specified flat glass downstairs and curved glass up.

Bury's first Fleetlines arrived from Falkirk accompanied by two even rarer (for Lancashire) Y-types on AEC Reliance chassis to supplement a saloon-operated, linked series of outer-suburban routes southeast and southwest of Bury, which had been initiated way back in 1957. This arrival of 32 new buses, a third of the Corporation fleet, in 12 months, was caused by the need to clear out the immediate postwar purchases — which had themselves replaced both wartime arrears and, in 1949, the surviving trams — and also to dispose of Lenny, the sick man of Bury, who joined a Welsh independent.

The radical change of manufacturers between the two batches of double-deckers was doubtless caused by a difference in tender prices — members of both batches achieved respectable ages (in the days of 50% new bus grant) of 15-16 years. But the new Manager, Norman Kay, was to move the body contracts for future batches closer to home — to East Lancs of Blackburn. The first fruits of this policy, in 1965, were six further Fleetlines with Sheffield-style bodies sporting a vertically-divided, curved pair of lower-deck windscreens — unusual but attractive. These were followed in 1966 by six more with peaked instead of rounded domes, and a single-piece curved screen.

Then came an aberration — four exposed-radiator PD2s with traditional forward-entrance bodies. These did not indicate a reversion from rear-engined buses but were bought for the Bolton via Breightmet service which traversed Bolton's Trinity Street station bridge, requiring a low axle weight; they were speedily followed by three dual-doored single-deck Fleetlines. The standee style was now fashionable and the remaining purchases before the SELNEC PTE took over were all dual-doored and East Lancs-bodied. There were three Atlanteans with rather elegant, slightly rounded styling, seven Fleetlines to the same specification but with angular slab-fronts and six more Fleetline single-deckers, almost identical to the first three. All of these were still in service in 1976, but I arrived just too late to see the Bedford J2 purchased in 1969 for a new route to Topping Fold estate.

Ramsbottom's fleet had consisted of 11 PD3s with East Lancs bodies and a solitary, second-hand Albion Nimbus (new to Halifax), bought for the tight turning-point in Holcombe village. In 1976 the latter passed to my father's employers, Thomas Preston Ltd, for use as a works bus — and the 1949-vintage Ramsbottom destination blind passed into the Howarth collection soon after. Legally, I might add — don't let the title mislead you, I'm keen on saving money but I didn't let that platform ticket incident lead me too far astray. By that time the 12 remaining Titans — eight survivors from Ramsbottom (6404-11) and the four Bury PD2s (6387-90) which were displaced after the Trinity Street bridge was strengthened — had gravitated to the interworked Bury-Ainsworth and Ainsworth-Radcliffe-Whitefield services, as these required a conductor to reverse them at Ainsworth terminus.

I was taught at Ainsworth Junior School for a few weeks, prior to the summer holidays and going on to secondary school from September, and the reversing manœuvres took place outside my classroom window

with throaty Leyland sound-effects. I can remember one day when, having noted each arrival's fleetnumber, I heard a bus draw up as the headmaster was making a speech to our class. With the temerity of the obsessed enthusiast I stealthily (but surely very obviously) got up, sidled to the window, got the number and reseated myself. What was I thinking of? My notes showed that the bus would return in an hour, yet I still risked punishment and humiliation.

As it happened, I was to spend the next seven years riding on the Ainsworth-Whitefield route, clocking up nearly 13,000 miles on the bus to school — many of them on 6411, the very last PD3 built — being whisked twice a day past the premises of that extraordinary coach operator, Tatlock's, whose fleet cannot be reviewed here but which deserves detailed coverage at a later date.

Top:
By 1969 a standard Bury 'look' was emerging, although the three dual-doored Atlanteans of that year had several internal features which did not appear anywhere else. The grace which the author once saw in these vehicles and which nearly tempted him into preservation is not apparent in this view, taken in Bury town centre.

Above:
Ramsbottom stuck firmly with East Lancs-bodied Titans to the very end. This 1967 example is representative of these typical Lancashire municipal purchases. The last one, indeed the last Titan built by Leyland in 42 years of production, was delivered to SELNEC in November 1969.

There were lots of numbers for me to collect because of all the 'foreigners' which were sent to Bury from their native GMT depots. Six Atlanteans with Bolton's shrouded bodystyle were allocated to Bury and, when these returned to their home patch, four Roe-bodied Atlanteans came from Oldham to replace them, being in turn replaced by nine (out of the 12 built) single-door Mancunians. An extra PD3 came from Stockport's final batch to spend a few months on the Ainsworth routes — i was most impressed by the translucent roof that gave an airy interior upstairs. The native standee Fleetlines were

withdrawn after 11 years' work and three ex-North Western Bristol REs of similar vintage with very smart Marshall bodywork arrived to cover their duties. But the best single-deckers were three nearly-new Leopards with ECW coach bodywork which were primarily used on the long route from Bury through Rawtenstall to Water, joint with Rossendale (whose normal rosterings were neat and well-turned-out maroon and cream East Lancs-bodied saloons).

Also to be seen working into Bury were ex-Rochdale Fleetlines with very plain, small-windowed Weymann bodywork which lacked any trace of styling (well, it was Orion-derived), and on the jointly-worked 35 trunk route from Manchester came Salford's standard Fleetlines, old-fashioned PD2/40s and occasional Manchester Atlanteans. Even in 1976 one Mancunian was still in red and white, albeit looking rather grubby. Bolton tended to send middle-aged Atlanteans to Bury, but then I discovered a new side to The Curse Of Shopping. As a 12-year-old, there were few things worse than trailing round C&A and British Home Stores with my mother. My feelings were reciprocated! What better for both parties, then, than to deposit me with notebook and pencil on a bench adjacent to, say, Great Moor Street in Bolton and abandon me indefinitely?

It worked for both sides and that excursion saw my notebook filled with all kinds of Boltonian exotica — Neepsend bodies, Liverpool-style PDR1s, which in subtle ways were not as stylish as Bury's, and huge 82-seat PDR2s (three of which were transferred to Bury's Ramsbottom outstation to cope with school journeys). I was particularly taken by the batch of Atlanteans with vast picture-windows, sloping pillars and dual doors, which looked very elegant with their chrome trim and white-on-green 'via' blinds. The latter Bolton speciality had originally started as white lettering on a red ground, to match the Corporation's maroon livery, but was frowned on by the police for showing red lights on the front of the vehicle. Coincidentally, many years later, Roy Marshall at Burnley & Pendle tried to introduce white-on-blue destination blinds (which give the best contrast for the human eye) but the Lancashire Constabulary outlawed this also. Too many cases of the 23 to Padiham being stopped to put out chip-pan fires, I suppose.

Top:
Also in 1969, Bolton was taking delivery of these rather more modern machines. Fifteen dual-doored Atlanteans with panoramic, raked windows represented the final fling of a distinctive bus design for the town. General Manager Ralph Bennett had moved from here to Manchester in 1965, and the bus pictured was a deliberately stylish rejoinder to Bennett's classy Mancunian.

Above:
Another town with a distinctive look to its buses was Oldham, which built up a large fleet of Roe-bodied Atlanteans. The accentuated peaks, high-pitched windscreen and high-mounted blinds specified by Oldham made for a top-heavy-looking vehicle, but the main thing for the Transport Committee was that it did not look like an Ashton or Rochdale bus.

South East Lancashire and North East Cheshire

I haven't yet mentioned the SELNEC/GMT purchases. Five Fleetlines ordered by Bury Corporation were delivered in 1972 with Northern Counties bodies to the new SELNEC standard design except for flat, featureless dash panels. This batch was followed by 10 from the first series of Park Royal-bodied Fleetlines in 1973 and then by dribs of Northern Counties-bodied Atlanteans and drabs of Fleetlines. GMT allocated new vehicles in batches of one or occasionally two, and all depots received both AN68s and Fleetlines pretty much at random, although one Manchester depot notoriously had a manager who did not favour the latter and all Daimlers delivered there were very rapidly transferred out.

Deliveries of standards slowly rose up from 7001, until one gloomy evening, when the highest number yet achieved was around 7810, I saw a vision whilst standing outside Radcliffe library. I had been to the library to restamp *Buses Annual 1976*, Roy Marshall's *PTE Buses in Camera* and Gavin Booth's Contractual Obligation Book of *The Classic Omnibus* (I believe that under the Public Amenities (Libraries) Regulations of 1973 all British libraries must stock at least one of Gavin's books — it's a good job they are so readable) and maybe this had affected me. Opposite me in the sodium lamplight, a brand new standard double-decker rolled up — number 8165. I pinched myself hard. Had I missed the delivery of 350 vehicles in a month? Hold that front page!

It turned out that there was a fairly rational explanation, based on late deliveries, dual-sourcing and cancelled orders, but I still remember that slightly dazed feeling. I wasn't nearly as surprised (although I did nearly fall off my bike) when, a couple of years later, GMT reverted from split, single-piece upstairs windscreens to a traditional, sturdy front pillar. The reason for this apparently retrograde step was Northern Counties'

change from steel to aluminium panelling as part of a general revision of the body structure, which had shown several weaknesses. The aluminium front domes turned out to be much more flexible than the steel ones, and I believe an upstairs windscreen bounced out (whoops), leading to the retrofitting of interior handrails all around the upstairs front windows and first bay, to brace the assemblage until a stronger basic design with beefed-up pillars could be adopted.

The service pattern at this stage was surprisingly underdeveloped. For several years, SELNEC made do with a dozen overlapping route number series before carrying out a wide-ranging renumbering scheme in 1974. This merged the Salford and Manchester route numbers into a single series, with the lowest numbers running west from Manchester into the Salford badlands and then increasing towards 199 in an arc sweeping anti-clockwise across southwest and south Manchester. The 2XX route numbers were used by the ex-North Western services that overlaid this pattern. Stockport's services were numbered from 300 upwards, and the arc then swept on

The MCW Metropolitans lived short but high-mileage lives, mainly on the misnamed Trans-Lancs Express. Its main function was as a series of interurban links rather than an hourly through service, but it was not duplicated even if all seats were taken, which quite often led to through passengers being turned away.

around Manchester with Ashton and Tameside services numbered from 330, Oldham services from 400, Rochdale services from 435, Bury services from 468, Bolton from 500, Leigh from 560 and Wigan from 600, with Lancashire United's services overlaying the northwest quarter of the conurbation in the range 550-675.

The route pattern consisted of a series of radial networks based on each town's original tramlines and frozen by the Road Traffic Act in 1930, running out from central bus stations (GMT was a great one for building new bus stations) and with the local networks connected by interurban routes from one bus station to the next. Today's pattern, which considers Greater Manchester as a homogenous whole, did not exist in the 1970s as there was political pressure to maximise employment and lots of short journeys and frequent layovers require more manpower than long, integrated, through routes. Moreover, inertia held a powerful grip over Britain, and local politicians were surprisingly powerful by today's standards. Changing the *status quo* was slow and painful, and in 1986/7 involved reinstating the long interurban express routes which had been discontinued at the Traffic Commissioner's insistence around 1930. Which goes to show that what goes around, comes around, as they say in these parts.

An albatross in the metal — an ex-SHMD dual-door Fleetline. This one is seen late in life as a hard-to-supervise OPO bus but they ran for many years as crew-operated, centre-entrance/front-exit buses so that the conductor could supervise the sliding door.

However, buses in 1977 were frequent and modern, free timetables and maps were plentiful, and fares were comparatively low. In particular, that summer I discovered the Saver Seven, a ticket giving me unlimited travel for seven days on all GMT buses and the county's railways, and I saved like fury to buy one. Fresh frae Bonnie Scotland, I was keen on anything with 'Saver' in the name and, whilst I didn't know what Grotton or Harpurhey looked like — I didn't even know how to pronounce them — I knew (thanks to the free maps) how to get there, and plotted my excursions assiduously as the summer holidays approached.

Day 1 : The Day of Two Thousand Resting Buses

Saver Seven validity commenced on a Sunday, which was rather a swizz as 95% of buses were tucked up in their depots on Sunday mornings back then and I would have been happy to pay rather less for a Saver Six. Nonetheless, full of expectation and processed cheese, I ground into Manchester by bus — no Sunday trains to Bury in 1977! — and explored the highways and railways of the southeast suburbs before making a long (and, frankly, tedious) sweep home from Stockport on the hourly 400 Trans-Lancs Express.

The 'Trans-Lancs Express' title, emblazoned on the 'via' blind, was a decided misnomer: the 400 trundled up the same urban streets as the normal services, stopped at a hundred traffic lights and never entered Lancashire. Prior to the 1974 boundary changes the majority of the

mileage had been on Lancastrian tarmac but with almost a third on Cheshire's. By now it was the Trans (or possibly Semi-Circum) Greater Manchester Limited Stop — but perhaps that wouldn't fit in the blind aperture. It was run by a batch of 10 MCW Metropolitans allocated to Ashton depot, imposing a vehicle change en route at Ashton bus station on many northbound journeys, as the thirsty Scania engines managed barely 6.5mpg and the buses needed frequent refuelling. This consumption rate was a problem on a round trip of 58 miles; or 64 miles on summer Sundays when the route was extended beyond

Stockport to run Bolton-Bury-Rochdale-Oldham-Ashton-Stockport-Manchester Airport. The Metropolitans accelerated smoothly to a cruise of 35mph, at which point their squishy air suspension allowed them to roll like the Jura ferry in a Force 8. What with the ride, the fuel consumption and electrolytic body-rot, GMT scrapped the entire batch on or before their seventh birthdays. But on the day in question all went well, conveying me from Stockport, home of Crossley Motors, through Oldham, home of Seddon Motors, and Rochdale, home of, er, Gracie Fields, back to Bury . . . um . . . very much the River Irwell's answer to Budapest.

Day 2 : Independence Day

Monday saw me set out for Lancashire United Transport territory, by way of Wigan. The ex-municipal fleet still looked to be retaining some independence and I rode on a Titan, 57, in the full Wigan Corporation livery of deep maroon and white with shaded gold fleetname, *sans* any sign of PTE ownership beyond the legal lettering. The local Corporation had clearly prevailed on ratepayer Northern Counties for all kinds of modifications to the standard bodies, and each batch of buses looked to be unique to the town.

From there I travelled south to Bryn and awaited an eastbound bus on route 1. This was an LUT/Merseyside joint route from St Helens to Atherton and, as I stood on Bryn's red-brick terraced street, an ex-St Helens PD2 passed westbound, clad in Verona green and cream. Sadly, I was not so fortunate, the eastbound bus turning out to be one of the very first Leyland Nationals received by Lancashire United, imposed by the new masters at Devonshire Street North, and in overall red with no relief colour. It rained in a bleak south Lancashire way as we whisked past Hindley depot, a long yard full of LUT oddments coming momentarily into view, but the clouds cleared as we came into Atherton.

Top:
Although Lancashire United was an early recipient of Fleetlines, front-engined vehicles soon reappeared once Guy realised that the Wulfrunian was not going to be a success and consequently reintroduced the Arab. This late-model Arab V, one of many Guy Arabs bought by LUT through the 1960s, is seen in Bolton when almost new.

Above:
Forced by the Government's new Bus Grant to buy rear-engined buses, LUT went to the extreme and bought 10 dual-door 'jumbos' which spent most of their career on the 582 Bolton-Atherton-Leigh trunk service. This one is fitted with the Videmat self-service farebox described in the text.

I grabbed a pasty (curse the title, I bought a pasty!) and noted a plethora of unlikely vehicles circling the town's gyratory system. Leopards, REs, LHs and RUs all had bodywork apparently intent on capturing the graceless style of the Class 504 EMU in road-going form — slab sides, high window-lines, two flat-front

Despite being a member of various express pools, LUT had some very odd ideas about what made a coach. The last fling in this direction was a batch of 10 Plaxton-bodied Bristol REs, which were in no way comparable with the Plaxton-bodied REs being delivered to the National Express fleet at that time. Au contraire. The batch was delivered in a reversed livery of grey with a red band, but was soon repainted into bus colours as shown.

windscreens and central rear emergency exits had been specified, giving that distinctive — unfashionable — LUT look. Several short-wheelbase Leopards were operating stage services in a livery with much more grey relief. I eschewed these to catch a Videmat-equipped Fleetline for the one-mile journey to Howe Bridge, spending an unnecessary 4p to get a large souvenir ticket bearing a photograph of the coins I had deposited in the nearside farebox.

At Howe Bridge, the company head office, I was able to obtain (purchase) a copy of the last independent issue of the LUT timetable book, complete with an impressive route map showing the sprawl of services bounded by Bolton, Manchester, Wigan and Warrington. The depot, on both sides of a busy road, contained a vast army of Arabs and Fleetlines of all vintages — some of the latter bearing fluted Daimler scroll badges, fully 4ft wide, across the dash panel. I still miss the independence of this very traditional operator, although it is clear that it could not have survived long after deregulation without radical changes.

Day 3: The Day of the King of the Road

On Tuesday I made my way to Rochdale, riding on the very traditional buses of that town which presumably had looked magnificent in the ivory and navy blue of long ago, but looked gawky and unprepossessing in orange. SELNEC went to considerable lengths to arrange the orange and white livery in the most attractive proportions, but these small-windowed, sheet steel-interiored buses had not aged well. I sniffed with the civic pride of a true citizen of Bury.

After trying rear-engined double- and single-deckers (the AEC Regents had already vanished) I poked my nose

into Yelloway's depot-cum-coach station, where lines of old Reliances and one or two new ones sat under cover, reflected in puddles of water which had penetrated the disintegrating overall roof. At the far end of this silent and largely empty space (similar to the Associated Motorways station at Cheltenham) sat an old man on a canvas chair, and I walked all the way across to ask permission to look around. He must have been in his 70s, swathed in a magnificent brown overcoat and cap, both trimmed in gold and embroidered with Yelloway's timeless logo, and he was profuse in his thanks for my small courtesy. I don't think anyone had paid him any more attention than the roof in recent years. Yelloway, *primus inter pares* on the road, is now just another memory.

I moved on from Rochdale to Oldham and found a very different scene. Oldham had spent heavily on new buses in the late 'sixties, filling its enormous garage at Wallshaw Place with long rows of Roe-bodied Atlanteans, fitted with letterbox-narrow upstairs windscreens and deep peaks, which looked dashing and modern. Ex-Ashton-under-Lyne routes ran into Oldham using very similar vehicles (on paper), but Ashton had specified round domes and curved screens to ape Alexander, and, whilst the panels and glass shapes were largely the same, the look of the two former fleets was very different.

Day 4 : The Day of the Bus Designed by Committee

On the following day I explored those long routes which thread off into the steep-sided Pennine valleys east of Manchester which had been partially the territory of North Western Road Car and partially that of the Stalybridge, Hyde, Mossley & Dukinfield Joint Board. These routes tended to be irregular, making connections in places like Delph and Carrbrook a little chancy and, even today, whilst I can cross 'S' and 'H' off my list, I am not entirely certain that I have fully explored 'M' and 'D'.

The biggest surprise of the day came in Ashton bus station, where, in amongst the ageing Titans and ex-SHMD Bristol/Northern Counties saloons, I found an amazing contraption. It was another Daimler Fleetline but with the front sawn off so that there was only room ahead of the front wheels for a narrow two-leaf door, marked 'Exit Only'. Behind the front wheels was a sliding doorway with an entrance divided into an upstairs entry (left) and a downstairs entry (right) channel. Overall, this stubby creation was of functional mid-sixties styling, but the lower-deck windscreen consisted of two huge, oversized square panes set at a pronounced dihedral. It turned out that there were several of these albatrosses around, SHMD having bought 10 of them in the late 'sixties, but they had short lives as they were unsuitable and short of seats, even after conversion for OPO.

Afterwards I begged the driver of a Manchester-bound Mancunian to call out when we got to Droylsden, Edge Lane — which he did, the sterling chap, after a three-mile drag down a wide, endless road carved through a nondescript, urban sprawl, pockmarked by newsagencies and hoardings for Guinness and rolling tobacco. My reason for descending into this unprepossessing landscape arrived almost instantly — an open-platform AEC Regent V in dull, dark maroon lined in turquoise. This was Mayne's traditional Droylsden-Manchester service (nowadays hugely expanded), and several Regents still remained in use despite

the recent arrival of five Roe-bodied Daimler Fleetlines. These latter P-registered vehicles, although comprising the most respected body and chassis combination of the day, led strangely short lives, most being withdrawn (and in some cases scrapped) by Mayne when 11-13 years old, replaced by 15-year-old DMSs cast off by London Transport. It was noticeable that Mayne's next new double-deckers, in 1978-80, were Gardner-engined VRTs, not Fleetlines. Three of the then-nearly-new Daimlers were seen as we approached Manchester from its least attractive direction, to terminate in strangely desolate Stevenson Square. A whisk around the city centre on a rough, raucous and Rabelaisian Seddon midibus took me to Victoria and the train home.

Day 5: The Day It All Started Getting Blurred

Of Thursday's excursion to south Manchester only a couple of features stand out. One was the gleaming Silver Jubilee bus, one of six brand-new GMT standards delivered in overall silver with a metallic purple waistband, parked amongst over two dozen other vehicles at Southern Cemetery, deep in Manchester's suburbs. Vehicles congregated here as there was a large canteen adjacent to several termini athwart the Princess Parkway, and even at 10am there was clearly a lot of tea being drunk.

Altrincham, reached by a speedy Cheshire Lines DMU from Oxford Road, was awhirl with Leyland Nationals, one of which took me pitching round the smart semi-lined suburb of Hale Barns, the howl of the 510 engine echoing amidst the ivy-clad porticoes. And towards evening, boarding a Manchester-bound bus but unsure of the terminus, I said to the driver 'St Peter's Square?' 'Is he?' he replied with a glint. 'Is he really?' Ah, the old ones . . .

GMT took delivery of six standard Atlanteans painted in a special livery of silver with a purple waist to celebrate HM The Queen's Silver Jubilee in 1977. These six rotated amongst the 20 GMT depots. The 'PS' sticker indicates this one was running from Manchester, Princess Road.

Day 6: The Day Disillusion Set In

Friday saw a dramatic change of scene to the limitless Vicwardian brickery of Salford. Weaste depot, its surrounding streets either boarded or bulldozed, was a squalid ruin full of tired half-cabs with external winding gear to change the destination. The real Coronation Street had already gone but the people looked like refugees from the TV series, all headscarves and Capstan full-strength. Grimy terraces were still widespread, but the shopping-trolley-girt tower blocks were the traffic generators that fuelled the many buses.

I sat on upstairs front seats and worried about having to get off. But, keeping a tight grasp of my Marmite sandwiches, I survived and a shiny, red Lancashire United Guy Arab IV with open rear platform took me off to Leigh, where LUT had a little 'fifties fantasy of a bus station, all curved glass and cantilevered canopy, 20 yards from the larger, less stylish one of GMT. The latter's Leigh garage ran a fascinating assortment of AEC Renowns and Metro-Scanias, and one of the latter hurtled me sportively round the town's eastern suburbs, weaving between the parked cars like a Grand Slalom skier and passing the low-roofed depot which required the allocation of single-deckers rather than GMT standards. Afterwards, a long, slow LUT journey wound me tortuously back through Pendlebury and Windsor Crescent to the Stygian gloom of the terminus known as Manchester Greengate — but which was actually a pair of tunnels underneath Exchange station (technically in Salford) and surely where Dirty Harry would go to duel with mobsters. Still, there were plenty of buses from

Greengate terminus to the true centre of Manchester. At least deregulation has eliminated this sort of nonsense and buses today go to where passengers want. Which is to say, they don't go to Greengate any more.

Day 7: Can I have some money back, please?

By Saturday I was tired. Tired of trains, grimy terraces, stale cigarette smoke, stout adverts and adverts for stout. Even tired of buses. I had seen the sights, experienced the sounds and could navigate from Brookbottom to Dangerous Corner without a bus map. I wanted to stay in and read the latest Gavin Booth.

I pulled the sheets over my head. I should have been out exploring, but on the seventh day I rested. Roll on the Saver Six.

Greater Manchester Transport

Bury District Timetable

January 1976 until further notice

10p

Left:
Thriving East Manchester independent Mayne took five of these Roe-bodied Fleetlines in 1976, but they had strangely short lives. This one lasted longest of all, being scrapped by Mayne in 1990. The maroon and aqua livery was phased out after this batch in favour of the coach scheme of crimson and cream.

Left:
Salford's fleet appeared very old-fashioned to my youthful eyes, with over 100 of these obsolescent Titan PD2/40s delivered during the 'sixties. Note the external winding frame — short conductors stood on the radiator dumb-iron to change the destination blinds. The broad pillars above the front entrance stiffened an area of potential weakness and eliminated the need for non-standard-sized windows.

THE *TWIN-STEER* BEDFORD

The 21st century starts with three-axle coaches having their twin axles at the rear. But it wasn't always that way, and one of the most successful three-axle designs in the UK was the 1960s twin-steer Bedford VAL. Kevin Lane illustrates a selection.

Right:
An early style of Plaxton-bodied VAL, seen operating for Kavanagh of Urlingford in 1976, long after its first flush of youth. It had been new to Skill's of Nottingham in 1964 and like all early VALs was powered by a Leyland engine.
Kevin Lane collection

Below:
Pride of the fleet of Leon of Finningley in 1967 was this Plaxton-bodied VAL, seen at that year's Blackpool coach rally. VAL coaches were 36ft long and typically seated between 49 and 52 people.
Kevin Lane collection

The original Duple body for the VAL was the Vega Major, with its reverse-sloping pillar towards the rear. New in 1966 to Rickards of Brentford, this VAL had fallen on hard times when photographed in Southampton in the ownership of the Poole Sea Cadet Corps. The roof rack was used to carry boats but, while the VAL has lost its polished wheeltrims, it still retains a full set of headrest covers.
Kevin Lane

Inset:
Duple was the other main coachbuilder to body the VAL, and later vehicles had this handsome style of Viceroy bodywork. Hants & Dorset was one of a small number of Tilling group companies to run VAL coaches. One is seen in Bournemouth in 1972.
Alec Swain/Kevin Lane collection

THE *TWIN-STEER*
BEDFORD

ORU 579G

GABRIEL WADE (South

Above:
Bedford was a major exporter in the 1960s and 1970s, and sold a few VALs overseas. Destinations included Australia, where Bass Hill Coaches of Sydney operated this VAL with CCMC body.
Kevin Lane collection

Right:
A Danish operator owned this left-hand-drive VAL with Soro bodywork. Note the separate door for the driver, rare on British coaches but common in continental Europe. Now, if the gent with the cigarette would kindly move to one side we'd get to see the VAL's twin front wheels. . .
Kevin Lane collection

THE *TWIN-STEER* BEDFORD

inset:
Weymann built one Topaz body on a VAL. It was in fact fitted to two different chassis and is seen here after being transferred to its second chassis, in which form it was bought by Rowson of Hayes. It was a 49-seater. The later Topaz II from Weymann was only marginally more successful than the unique original.
Kevin Lane collection

Harrington produced the angular Legionnaire body for the VAL. This one, new to Taylor of Meppershall in 1964, is seen in preservation at the 1984 Showbus rally at Woburn. Kevin Lane

THE *TWIN-STEER*
BEDFORD